BALTIC SEA

Lejre

GUNDESTRUP
CAULDRON

Biskupin

RAGSTONE HEAD

Manching

Danube River

Hallstatt

Ciumeşti

Magdalenska gora

Stična

MINER'S
BACKPACK

THRACE

BLACK SEA

ETRURIA

BRONZE CUIRASS

Rome

ILLYRIA

GALATIA

Ankara

Pergamon

Delphi

Athens

TIME® LIFE BOOKS

Cover: The head of a bronze statue of a Celtic god, created in the image of its worshipers, fixes the viewer with its one remaining inlaid blue-and-white glass eye. While this work shows Roman influence, the pure Celtic art style known as La Tène exuberantly manifests itself in the bronze face of a wooden shield used here as a background.

End paper: Painted on bark paper by artist Paul Breeden, the map shows the farthest reaches of the Celts in their third-century-BC heyday, when their sway extended from the British Isles in the north, south to Spain and northern Italy, and east as far as modern Turkey. Key archaeological discoveries are marked by artifacts. Breeden also painted the images accompanying the timeline on pages 158-159.

CELTS:
EUROPE'S PEOPLE
OF IRON

Time-Life Books is a division of TIME LIFE INC.

PRESIDENT and CEO: John M. Fahey Jr.

EDITOR-IN-CHIEF: John L. Papanek

TIME-LIFE BOOKS

MANAGING EDITOR: Roberta Conlan

Executive Art Director: Ellen Robling
Director of Photography and Research: John Conrad Weiser
Senior Editors: Russell B. Adams Jr., Dale M. Brown, Janet Cave, Lee Hassig, Robert Somerville, Henry Woodhead
Director of Technology: Eileen Bradley
Director of Editorial Operations: Prudence G. Harris
Library: Louise D. Forstall

PRESIDENT: John D. Hall

Vice President, Director of Marketing: Nancy K. Jones
Vice President, New Product Development: Neil Kagan
Vice President, Book Production: Marjann Caldwell
Production Manager: Marlene Zack

Library of Congress Cataloging in Publication Data
Celts: Europe's people of iron / by the editors of Time-Life Books.
    p. cm. (Lost civilizations)
    Includes bibliographical references and index.
    ISBN 0-8094-9029-3
    1. Celts I. Time-Life Books. II. Series.
D70.C45 1994
940'.04916—dc20   94-10175
                                      CIP

LOST CIVILIZATIONS

SERIES EDITOR: Dale M. Brown
Administrative Editor: Philip Brandt George

Editorial staff for *Celts: Europe's People of Iron*
Art Director: Bill McKenney
Picture Editor: Marion Ferguson Briggs
Text Editors: Charlotte Anker (principal), Russell B. Adams Jr., Charles J. Hagner
Associate Editors/Research-Writing: Constance B. Contreras, Mary Grace Mayberry
Senior Copyeditors: Mary Beth Oelkers-Keegan (principal), Anne Farr
Picture Coordinator: David Herod
Editorial Assistant: Patricia D. Whiteford

Special Contributors: Marfé Ferguson-Delano, Laura Foreman, Ellen Galford, Donál K. Gordon, Jim Hicks, Michael T. Kerrigan, David S. Thomson (text); Douglas J. Brown, Tom DiGiovanni, Ylann Schemm (research/writing); Roy Nanovic (index).

Correspondents: Elisabeth Kraemer-Singh (Bonn), Christine Hinze (London), Christina Lieberman (New York), Maria Vincenza Aloisi (Paris), Ann Natanson (Rome). Valuable assistance was also provided by: Nihal Tamraz (Cairo), Barbara Gevene Hertz (Copenhagen), Ian Mills (Harare), Peter Hawthorne (Johannesburg), Judy Aspinall (London), Saskia Van de Linde (Netherlands), Dan Donnelly (New York), Ann Wise (Rome), Robert Kroon (Switzerland), Traudl Lessing (Vienna), Bogdan Turek (Warsaw).

The Consultants:
Frederick C. Suppe is a professor at Ball State University in Indiana, where he specializes in the history and cultures of all the Celtic peoples. He has written widely on Celtic religion and warfare and frequently lectures on Celtic folklore and the legends of King Arthur.

Peter S. Wells has participated extensively in European Iron Age archaeological excavations, including Heuneburg and Manching in Germany. He has also directed digs at three locations in Bavaria, among them Kelheim, the site of an ancient Celtic oppidum, or fortified town. At the University of Minnesota, where he teaches archaeology, his focus is European prehistory, particularly the Iron Age.

This volume is one in a series that explores the worlds of the past, using the finds of archaeologists and other scientists to bring ancient peoples and their cultures vividly to life.

CELTS:
EUROPE'S PEOPLE
OF IRON

By the Editors of Time-Life Books

TIME-LIFE BOOKS, ALEXANDRIA, VIRGINIA

CONTENTS

A GREAT PEOPLE MALIGNED BY HISTORY

Lime-thickened hair, a flowing mustache, and a heavy neck ring called a torque mark this Iron Age man as a Celt. This stylized stone carving from the second century BC is one of the few images of a Celt to come down to modern times.

Wood had no business inside a modern peat-shredding machine, so operator Andy Mould plucked the soggy piece from the conveyor belt and playfully tossed it in the direction of a co-worker. The "wood" missed and fell to the ground, shedding its mantle of peat on impact and presenting the two astonished men with a human right foot and a portion of the lower leg to which it was attached. For Andy Mould, working in the peat bogs of Lindow Moss outside of Manchester in northwest England, the grisly discovery, which occurred on August 1, 1984, was hardly shocking. A year earlier Mould had stopped the conveyor belt in order to remove a similar lump of peat that, once cleaned, turned out to be part of a human skull. Forensic scientists quickly determined that the skull was that of a 30- to 50-year-old woman, and police investigators wasted little time in reopening the still-unsolved case of a local homemaker who had vanished from the Lindow Moss area some 23 years earlier.

Confronted with this new evidence and convinced that his luck had at last run out, the woman's husband promptly owned up to the crime. Only later did archaeologists at Oxford University finally get around to carbon-dating the skull. The results must surely have given the murderer reason to regret his hasty confession, since the tests showed that the skull was not that of his dead spouse after all. It belonged to a woman who had lived and died sometime around the first century AD.

Given its potential as additional evidence, either criminally or archaeologically, the newly recovered foot was also brought to the attention of the local police, who told a newspaper reporter about it; he in turn notified Rick Turner, the Cheshire County archaeologist. Within a day of the find, Turner arrived on the scene, where he spied a flap of leathery skin protruding from the cut face of the bog. Subsequent excavations revealed the upper half of the naked body of a bearded man. Facedown, its head tucked birdlike into its right shoulder, the corpse proved to be remarkably well pre-

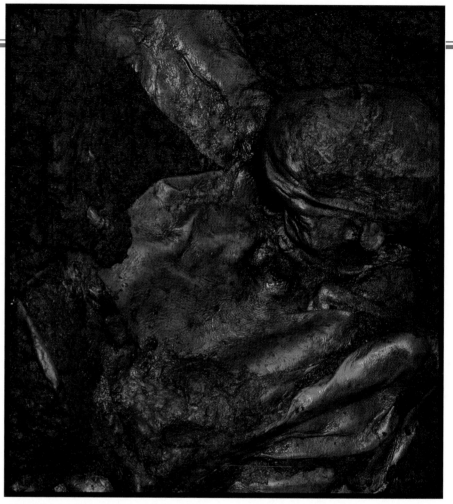

Head, face, and body squashed and distorted after 2,000 years of burial, the human sacrifice known as Lindow man lies as found on his back in a peat bog near Lindow Moss in the English Midlands. The victim retained his mustache and beard, though both were turned red by the acid from the decomposing moss that also preserved and tanned his skin.

served. The highly acidic, oxygen-starved environment of the bog had effectively inhibited oxidation and stifled the growth of decay-causing bacteria. (Four years later the skin of Lindow man's buttocks, part of his left leg, most of his right thigh, and the ends of the femur turned up. Only his left foot remains missing.)

The torso was dubbed Lindow man by scientists, but promptly nicknamed Pete Marsh by the media. Like any of Egypt's methodically embalmed pharaohs surviving into modern times, Lindow man was an ambassador of a vanished civilization. In all probability he was a Celt, a participant in an Iron Age culture that once held sway over much of Europe. As warriors, traders, and settlers, Celts had fought, traded, and settled in all directions: through what is today France, Spain, and Portugal to the roaring Atlantic; north to the wet, chill islands of Britain and Ireland; south over dizzying Alpine passes into the fertile valleys of northern Italy; and east to the Balkans and Greece where they would cross the Bosporus into Asia Minor to found a nation of their own—Galatia—in the heart of present-day Turkey. In their aggressive expansion across Europe between the seventh and first centuries BC, they often affected the course of ancient history. Various tribes of Celts sacked pre-Imperial Rome, hastened the decline of the Etruscans, raided Delphi in Greece, and according to one account, even mounted a coup d'état in Egypt.

Yet the image of the Celts as fierce fighters who took the heads of enemy warriors as trophies has tended to obscure their peaceable side: They were also skilled artisans, ironworkers, carpenters, traders, miners, and builders. While they left no great temples, no ruins of once splendid cities, no monuments to now forgotten kings, among them were artists of uncommon style and sensibility, as numerous archaeological finds have demonstrated. Indeed, Celtic accomplishments in this area prompted the 20th-century Italian archaeologist Sabatino Moscati to call the Celts "the world's first abstractionists, the first true moderns." What is more, they were an articulate people, famous for the eloquence of their bards and priests. But most of all, they were farmers. While the sons of aristocrats and their followers might be off fighting, most Celts quietly worked their lands and counted their wealth in the number of cattle they owned.

Lindow man turned out to be a true relic of his era and culture. In the weeks and months that followed his discovery, his torso was rigorously examined inside and out. The body was x-rayed and autopsied, given numerous computed tomography (CT) and magnetic resonance imaging (MRI) scans, and subjected to detailed endoscopic procedures. Its blood was typed, its hair and nails were scanned under an electron microscope, and tissue and bone samples were radiocarbon dated. Even the contents of Lindow man's stomach and small intestine were scrutinized.

The various test results shed light on a corner of the distant past. At the time of his death Lindow man had been in the prime of life, perhaps only 25 or 30 years old. Except for a touch of arthritis and a routine case of intestinal worms, he was in good health. Average in height for his time, he had stood a muscular five foot six and had carried type-O blood, probably the most common blood group among his Celtic contemporaries.

Forensic specialists created this lifelike reconstruction of Lindow man. Working from radiographs and photographs of his crushed head, they re-created his skull in clay and cast it in plaster, then applied clay to the plaster in an approximation of the soft tissue. Next they made a wax cast of the model and, in the final steps, added glass eyes, ruddy skin tones, and dark brown hair that duplicated the fine, soft texture of the surviving samples.

A STEP-BY-STEP SCIENTIFIC ANALYSIS OF LINDOW MAN'S END

In a kind of unfolding horror story, forensic examination of Lindow man revealed the grisly details of his ritualized death. As a first step, x-rays were made immediately after the removal of his well-preserved body from its 2,000-year-old resting place, the peat bog of Lindow Moss in northwest England. They showed that acids present in the water from decaying vegetable matter had robbed the bones of their calcium, making it difficult for the examiners to differentiate soft tissue from hard.

When scientists gathered in London to study Lindow man, they had only fuzzy x-ray images of an arm bone, some vertebrae and ribs, and a skull to go by. The researchers knew that the body was ancient. In fact, initial radiocarbon dating suggested that the cadaver might be at least 1,000 years old. All else about the victim—age, cause of death, even whether the body was really that of a male—awaited analysis.

Removing the clinging peat by hand and with brushes and jets of water, the researchers first exposed the left arm, then the right, and finally the head, which they found compressed and wrenched down and toward the right shoulder. A beard and mustache demonstrated that the subject was indeed male.

Though skin on Lindow man's head and elsewhere bore

A scientist bathes Lindow man with distilled water while others inspect his back. Required to keep the body from drying out during examination, the fluid was boiled, chilled, and changed often to inhibit decay-causing microorganisms.

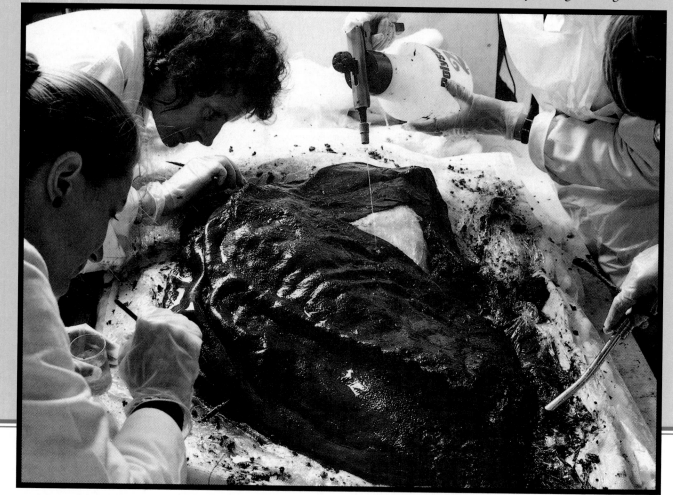

signs of postmortem sagging and tearing, the scalp offered investigators their first clues as to the cause of death: a pair of lacerations, each more than an inch long, arranged in a V near the crown of the skull.

Special soft-tissue x-rays called xeroradiographs displayed bone fragments driven deep into the skull cavity, hinting that a narrow-bladed, penetrating instrument had been used to produce the crushing blows. Yet these appear not to have been immediately fatal. Viewing the edges of the wounds under a dissecting microscope, the examiners discerned swelling, a sign that the victim, though no doubt un-

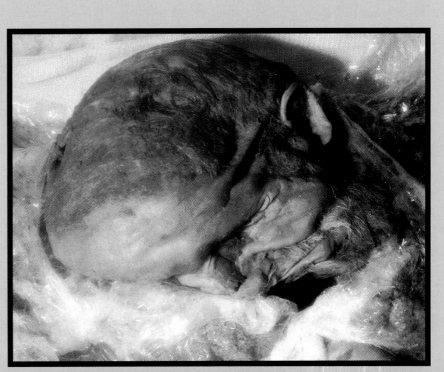

Lindow man's lower left second molar testifies to the force with which he must have been struck on the head. The blows slammed his jaws together, experts surmise, chipping the tooth.

The infrared photograph above and the xeroradiograph below show fractures in Lindow man's skull and his left rear ribs (arrow). Because the breaks on the crown of the skull were paired with lacerations in the skin, the forensic experts came to the conclusion that he was given two sharp blows from behind, probably administered in quick succession, while he was either standing or kneeling. The examiners thought that the broken ribs were most likely caused by a heavy blow, perhaps delivered by the executioner with his bent knee.

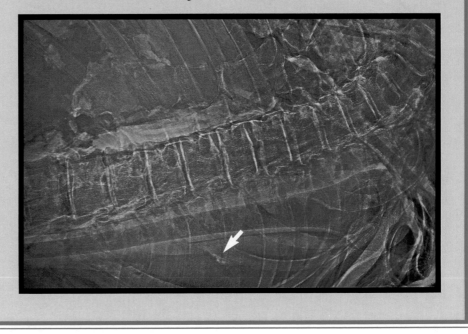

conscious, survived the assault.

Death came later, as one of the investigators discovered as he gently extended his fingers through a postmortem opening in the back of the neck. Looking to explain the head's odd position, he felt for the spine but instead found a gap between the third and fourth cervical vertebrae—evidence of a broken neck. A thin strand of sinew tied around Lindow man's throat—visible in the autopsy photograph below—was the likely means by which the injury was inflicted. By inserting a stick between the neck and this sinew cord and then turning it forcefully, the executioner would have snapped Lindow man's spine and cut off his breathing. Twists found in a portion of the cord behind the head may well have resulted when the sinew was tightened.

But a deep two-inch stab wound discovered just above the cord on the right side of the throat suggests a gorier purpose. Provided the carotid arteries had not been choked off, the garrote would have backed up blood in the jugular vein, causing the vein to spurt violently when severed by a knife—a sight intended perhaps to please the gods to whom Lindow man apparently was being sacrificed.

With a mirror in place at lower left, a researcher gently raises Lindow man's bearded chin, exposing the stab wound on the right side of his throat and the loop of dark sinew, visible at center, found just beneath it.

Curiously, for a man who had lived in so rough-and-tumble an age, Lindow man's nails were beautifully manicured, their surfaces unblemished by the telltale nicks and scratches of a laborer. Most telling of all, however, were the actual circumstances of Lindow man's death, since all the evidence seemed to indicate that he had not just died but had been sacrificed.

His wounds and the presence of a garrote still twisted tightly around his neck revealed that Lindow man had had a particularly gruesome end: He had been clubbed, strangled, and stabbed before being plunged into a bog pool. There he had lain for nearly 2,000 years, first submerged and then entombed in rapidly forming peat, until his chance encounter with the turf-cutting machine.

The evidence produced by the examination of Lindow man's corpse led to a theory that he had been a victim—probably a willing one—of a ritual: In a society where nakedness seems to have been part of sacred rites, he had apparently gone calmly to his death clad only in a fox-fur armband. The careful evaluation of his last meal seemed to confirm the ceremonial nature of his demise. His stomach contents were put through a high-tech procedure called electron spin resonance, or ESR, a technique that allows scientists to trace the "thermal history" of a material, in this case precisely how long the meal had been cooked and at what temperature. Shortly before his death Lindow man had eaten a small amount of bread baked quickly at high heat. Carbonized grain fragments indicated that at least some of the bread had been baked even more quickly at a still higher temperature, perhaps deliberately charred.

The significance of scorched bread was hinted at in oral traditions written down long after Lindow man's death, in Scotland, Wales, and Ireland. These accounts suggest a time when the victims of Celtic sacrifices were chosen by lot after drawing a portion of similarly blackened bread. Lindow man's gut also contained a few grains of mistletoe pollen. This information deepened the suspicion of some scholars that his death had been part of a dark ritual, since mistletoe was highly regarded by the Celts for its medicinal powers and was especially prized by Celtic priests, the mysterious Druids, as a potent source of magic.

Yet with all this probing of Lindow man, many intriguing questions remained, even the date of his death. The stratum in which his body appeared indicated that he had died in the third century BC, when the Celts were at the apex of their influence. But later carbon-

14 testing of his remains sped the date forward to the first century AD, when Celtic Britain was succumbing to the Romans. Scholarly opinion remains split between the two appraisals.

Although the identity of Lindow man and the events surrounding his demise are still open to conjecture, at least one authority, the British Celtic scholar Anne Ross, has hazarded a series of hypotheses: First, she suggests that the meticulously manicured Celt was neither artisan nor farmer but was in all likelihood a member of the Celtic aristocracy, perhaps even a Druid, a term used both for Celtic scholars who memorized such diverse material as genealogy, law, history, and religious and spiritual lore and for those in this group responsible for carrying out specific religious functions. Lindow man's high-born status may have singled him out for a special

Balanced on one knee, a Celtic warrior wearing a torque, a helmet, and little else prepares to hurl a now vanished spear in this small bronze made by a Roman sculptor in the third century BC. The Celts horrified neighboring peoples by their ferocity and by going into battle naked. The Greek historian Strabo noted that "the whole race is madly fond of war."

death at a particular time of year—probably Beltane, one of four main Celtic feasts—at a specially chosen place, secluded Lindow Moss.

His violent triple death, according to this theory, was a carefully choreographed ritual intended to propitiate three different Celtic gods, each of whom required a particular form of sacrifice. And the sacrifice of Lindow man could have been a desperate act in terrible times—a last-ditch effort on the part of the Druids to secure the help of the gods in staving off the Celts' final subjugation by the Romans. Other archaeologists believe these speculations stretch the evidence too far, providing, at best, a set of hypotheses for further archaeological research.

Lindow man is arguably the best known and most studied of some 2,000 ancient Europeans who met their fates in a bog where their bodies encountered the preservative effects of the highly acidic peat. Such remains have provided a windfall for modern researchers *(pages 10-12)*. Indeed, the circumstances of Lindow man's discovery were repeated two and a half years afterward when, on the same conveyor belt, workers found part of the back and the spine of yet another human being. During the next few days, some 70 pieces of this body were pulled from railway wagons where peat, previously excavated, had been packed.

Fitting together the parts of the corpse

Brandishing the severed head of a defeated enemy, a warrior of the Picts—Celts of northern Scotland—exults after a victory in a 16th-century watercolor by English artist John White, who followed descriptions of the Picts found in ancient sources. Proof that Celts did wear blue body paint came in 1987 with the discovery of another naked male corpse in the same bog that yielded Lindow man; microscopic traces of blue remained on the skin.

15

like a jigsaw puzzle, the investigators learned it was that of a young man of about 22, with the unusual feature of having two thumbs on each hand. Buried naked, as was his predecessor, his tissue was at least as well preserved. Scholars believe that he was also a sacrificial victim. Two carbon-14 laboratories have set the date of his death as sometime between the second and fourth centuries AD. He had been decapitated, and there was a good deal of searching for the head, but in vain. The researchers wondered if the skull that had turned up four years earlier may, in fact, have belonged not to a woman as they originally thought but instead to this Iron Age man, acknowledging that it is difficult to identify gender with only a skull to examine.

Devotees of Celtic lore were abuzz with excitement when later laboratory evidence revealed that Lindow III—as the second corpse came to be called—was painted with a blue-green mix of clay and copper. It was the first hard evidence in nearly two millennia that confirmed the observations of such Romans as the poet Ovid and the conqueror Julius Caesar, who had written that Celtic warriors painted their bodies blue before battle or religious rites.

T racing the Celts through their material remains has not proven easy, as the story of Lindow man demonstrates. Nor has any archaeological discovery shed a great deal of light on their origins. In the early part of the first millennium BC the Celts began leaving traces that distinguish them from the late Bronze Age European civilization known as Urnfield. Cremating their dead, the Urnfield people buried the ashes in pottery urns found in cemeteries throughout Europe. As burial practices changed, the Celts buried the bodies of their elite in wooden chambers topped by mounds that sometimes reached 300 feet in diameter and 42 feet in height. All the goods necessary for a cozy afterlife accompanied the dead into these vaults.

The Celts in some sense may be considered the forebears of today's Irish, Welsh, English, French, Spanish, Swiss, Austrian, northern Italian, and various other western and central European citizens, but the heredity is purely cultural. DNA tests using skeletal material and tissue samples from bodies found in European bogs are still in their infancy, but so far they have been unable to document any significant continuity between ancient corpses and people living today. This is hardly surprising in view of the fact that no genetic ties have been found that connect the prehistoric DNA samples with one

Fashioned in bronze by learned Druids of ancient Gaul to keep track of the seasons and the proper times for sacred festivals, the almost 2,000-year-old Coligny calendar—represented here by a detail—is considered one of the oldest documents in the Celtic language, although it was written in borrowed Roman characters. Its columns numbered the days and months in a five-year cycle that reflected with remarkable accuracy the phases of the sun and the moon, showing the Celts had a sophisticated knowledge of celestial movements. The holes running down the center were for a wooden peg, used by the Druids to keep track of the passing days.

another. Such a lack of biological linkage strengthens the view of anthropologists that the Celts were not a group that sprang from a single biological heritage but a collection of tribes with a common culture, speaking dialects of a shared language.

Much of what is known today about the Celts has been learned through oral tradition, through the writings of their Greek and Roman contemporaries, through archaeological excavations of their settlements and burial sites found widely across Europe, and through the pre-Roman Celtic artifacts that have been recovered.

Although written about in their own time, the Celts themselves committed little to writing. In fact, they did not adopt a written language until they had been exposed to literate cultures. Then they borrowed the alphabets of their neighbors—the Etruscans, the Greeks, and especially the Romans—to write inscriptions on altars, weapons, monuments, and coins issued by Celtic kings or tribes. They also left a remarkable document called the Coligny calendar, after the place in France where it was found. Engraved on a bronze plate, it contained 16 lists of months. Later, the Irish Celts developed a form of writing known as ogam, a system of notches and slashes carved into stone and wood, used only for commemorating ceremonial events. But that was not until the fourth century AD. Since no written history of the Celts survives, their story was recounted largely by their adversaries, who inevitably displayed an enemy's bias in the telling.

The Greek and Roman writers of antiquity invariably described the Celts as a tall, well-built, fair-haired people, accomplished on horseback or in two-horse chariots, high-spirited, energetic, quarrelsome, boastful, and fearless in battle. They portrayed the warriors as washing their hair in lime and combing it back so that it stood out alarmingly. Said the ancient Greek writer Diodorus Siculus, "The hair is so thickened by this treatment that it differs in no way from a horse's mane." Broad, bristling mustaches completed the savage effect. It can come as no surprise that the authors depicted the Celts as bloodthirsty barbarians, much given to gluttony, drunkenness, and hedonism. One chronicler, the Greek historian Ephorus, writing in the fourth century BC, went so far as to number the Celts among the four great barbarian peoples of the known world, the others allegedly being the Libyans, Persians, and Scythians. Even so enlightened a figure as Plato could not resist skewering the Celts when he listed them as one of six peoples who were overly fond of drinking.

Greek writings contain the earliest known references to the Celts—called the Keltoi. Oldest of all is a sixth-century-BC sailing manual, since lost, parts of which were later paraphrased in a poem written in the fourth century AD by Rufus Festus Avienus, the Roman proconsul of Africa. Avienus places the Celts in France, Spain, and along the North Sea. The Greek geographer Hecataeus, writing around 500 BC, noted their presence in France, specifically on the outskirts of the Greek colony of Massilia, site of present-day Marseilles. A few decades later, the Greek historian Herodotus mentions them as living near the headwaters of the Danube River and "beyond the pillars of Hercules," or the Straits of Gibraltar.

The second-century-BC historian Polybius and his near contemporary, the Stoic philosopher Posidonius, provide the most complete portrait of the Celts as a people, each man enlivening his own account with information about Celtic dress, weapons, customs, and manners. Polybius, for example, vividly depicts the Celts' habit of fighting naked and their practice of taking the heads of their enemies. Similar observations occurred in Posidonius's writings, the originals of which, though now lost, were used extensively by such first-century-BC authors as Strabo and Diodorus Siculus, both Greeks.

Having more than once in their history set themselves on a collision course with Rome, the Celts were very much on the minds of Roman commentators. In his great history of Rome, Livy, writing in the first century BC, documents Rome's early encounters in the fourth century BC with the invaders his compatriots knew as Celtae, or Galli. But while his fellow historian Pompeius Trogus, a Romanized, Latin-speaking Gaul, attributes the Celts' lust for land to "internal discord and bitter dissension at home," Livy claims that the Celts had crossed the Alps into Italy for a more prosaic reason: They were "lured by the delicious fruits, and especially the wine."

Although such events as Livy described had taken place centuries before, he would live to see the Celts get their comeuppance when Julius Caesar defeated the Celtiberians in Spain, conquered the Gauls of western Europe, and then turned his legions loose on the Celtic tribes of Britain. Caesar's own version of these events found expression in *De Bello Gallico,* a book that is known to generations of Latin students, and a work that is at once a military history of his campaign in Gaul as well as a justification of his ruthless conquest of the

Spurring the mania for all things Celtic that swept across Europe in the last years of the 18th century was a literary and cultural upheaval known as the romantic movement. To the romantics, chief among them the renowned French philosopher Jean Jacques Rousseau, the Europe of their own time was suffocatingly effete and corrupt, burdened by the dead weight of the centuries. Far better, proponents believed, had been a pagan past, an earlier, simpler time when human beings had been happy, virtuous, and uncivilized—free to follow their natural impulses, untrammeled and uncorrupted by society's artificial laws and customs.

The Celts, whom many romantics saw as a mysterious but fascinatingly primitive people, clearly filled the bill as "nature's noblemen." Things Celtic became the rage, especially the Druids and their arcane religion, with its shadowy but no doubt unspeakable rituals. Collectors all over Europe began rifling likely sites, searching for Celtic treasures—and in the process hopelessly dispersing invaluable troves of artifacts.

The hysteria reached a point where virtually everything old was thought to be Celtic,

Celtic "barbarians" to the north.

Yet despite the prejudices he harbored against his enemy, Caesar remains today an important source of information about Celtic customs. He seemed fascinated by the Druids, bards, and *vates*—or augurers—who, as the sole keepers of their people's tradition, preserved in memory and passed on orally a body of lore and legend, law, and ritual. Caesar claimed that it took a novice Druid 20 years to master all he needed to know. With so much time and effort invested in this process, a full-fledged Druid would have been understandably reluctant to share his hard-won knowledge with the uninitiated. Such reserve might explain the Celts' early failure to write about their history and customs. Caesar hinted as much when he wrote that "the Druids think it unlawful to commit this knowledge of theirs to writing."

Only after the Celts adopted a writing system could some of the surviving Celtic oral traditions be set down. It was not until the eighth century AD that Irish monks, writing in Irish, recorded Christianized versions of the old stories. The earliest extant collection is a compendium of a number of these tales called *The Book of the Dun Cow*, which dates from around 1200 AD. Much of what found its way into the texts confirmed what the Greeks and Romans had been writing about the Celts all along. It seems that there were Celts who in fact relished a good battle, reveled in wine and feasting, and saw little point in anything so restrictive as monogamy.

A closer reading of these Irish and Welsh tales reveals the outlines of a Celtic culture the Greeks and Romans had never quite understood: A picture emerges of the religious Celt whose nakedness in battle is a kind of prayer, invoking the protection of the gods. There is also the gracious Celt, to whom every stranger is a guest, and the wise Celt, whose civilization was more advanced than its detractors would acknowledge. The delight the Celts allegedly took in lopping off the heads of their enemies was misunderstood. Not only was it an

Crowds of people, supposedly Celts, flock to worship at Stonehenge in this 1815 drawing executed under the spell of Celtomania. As a matter of fact, construction of the massive megalith in southern England was actually started around 2000 BC, well over a thousand years before the rise of the Celts—who in any case never erected a comparable stone structure.

from Stone Age barrows and burial mounds to Roman forts and the great megaliths such as Stonehenge *(above)* that rise mysteriously throughout northern Europe. It was not until the latter half of the 19th century that more careful and scientific archaeology would manage to sort out the confusion and at last begin to elucidate the real history and actual achievements of the Celts.

act of heroic triumph; it was also a way of paying respect to the reputation of the defeated enemy. And it may have been a means of possessing his soul and of using it to ward off evil.

The Celts left a linguistic legacy of another sort. Roots and endings of Celtic origin such as *dun*, meaning fort, were planted in the names of some Celtic places—London, for example—allowing linguists to trace the patterns of Celtic expansion northward and westward from central Europe. Celtic names crop up as far afield as Austria and Ireland. The Rhine bears a Celtic name, as do many rivers and lakes in western and central Europe. Celtic words and names written in the Latin alphabet, found among inscriptions in formerly Celtic areas, have helped tie local dialects to a common Celtic tongue. Paris, Belgium, Switzerland—or Helvetia, as it is sometimes called—all owe their names to the Celtic tribes known as the Parisii, the Belgae, and the Helvetii.

Oddly enough, not until the 16th and 17th centuries AD did scholars establish a link between the Celtic languages of old and more modern forms of these languages—Irish, Manx, Welsh, Cornish, Breton, and Gaelic, which is a Scottish form of Celtic, as well as some dialects of France, Spain, and northern Italy. At that time, the Welshman Edward Lhuyd and the Scotsman George Buchanan, both linguists, used classical sources to prove that the people of Ireland and Britain were of Celtic origin and that the languages of Ireland, Wales, Brittany,

and Cornwall had a common Celtic root. Until then the term Celt had been applied only to the Celtic peoples of the European continent, not to the tribes of Britain and Ireland, and it had never been used to describe the languages spoken by the Celts.

Despite these scholarly efforts, the word Celt did not come into widespread use until the romantic movement of the 18th century, triggered by an outbreak of "Celtomania." Both in the British Isles and on the Continent the popular imagination was seized by a fascination with Europe's pagan past, by an infatuation with all things Celtic, and by an obsession with the obscure rituals of the Druids. In such an atmosphere, fact was often embroidered into fantasy, ancient burial sites and fortresses became the backdrop for all manner of baseless speculation, and the Celt was idealized as Europe's own "noble savage." There was little to restrain the imagination, since historical sources and linguistic evidence proved scant. It was, complained one Danish antiquarian in 1806, as if "everything which has come down to us from heathendom is wrapped in a thick fog."

Penetrating that fog became the task of archaeology, which in the 19th century was making its own transition from the gentlemanly domain of antiquarians and treasure collectors to a genuine science. In fact, the sudden surge of interest in the Celtic past gave impetus to that development. But archaeology still had a long way to go before it could rightly be called a science. In the meantime Europe's Celtomaniacs undertook their own haphazard fieldwork in what soon became a mad race to profit from Europe's prehistoric past.

Leading the race were Europe's major museums, many of which hired local peasants to carry out hurried excavations. Other farmers robbed Celtic graves and sold the plunder to private collectors. In the Champagne region of France alone, an area notably rich in Celtic burials, as many as 50,000 graves were pillaged in the second half of the 19th century. During the same period, antiquarians, scientists, private collectors, and farmers alike crawled over sites in Switzerland, hauling in hoards of Celtic materials during what some called the "harvest time of archaeology" but which others decried as "a chaotic treasure hunt."

In an effort to apply some order to the disorganization that characterized the early pursuit of prehistoric antiquities, the Danish antiquarian Christian Jurgenson Thomsen divided what he referred

Its cover crowded with supposedly Celtic objects, an 1892 German study titled History of Man According to Present-Day Science *reveals the seriousness with which Iron Age remains were beginning to be treated after Celtomania fired interest in the prehistoric peoples of Europe. Such treatises encouraged the serious excavation of Bronze and Iron Age sites, helping to stave off their destruction by amateur archaeologists and treasure seekers.*

to as "the heathen time" into three successive ages, named for the primary material used in crafting the artifacts of each period—stone, bronze, and iron. First used by Thomsen in 1819 to classify the artifacts in the Copenhagen Museum, the system was not published in book form until 1836. While simple in theory, this patterning of ancient time periods, described by one scholar as "the cornerstone of modern archaeology," revolutionized the study of Europe's prehistory.

With that cornerstone in place, the stage was set for the discovery, in 1846 and 1857 respectively, of two of the most important Iron Age sites in Europe: The first was at Hallstatt, an ancient cemetery in Austria, and the second was at La Tène, a probable votive site of later vintage located along the shores of Switzerland's Lake Neuchâtel. Like previously discovered Celtic sites, Hallstatt and La Tène would be extensively excavated by amateur archaeologists. Yet these digs would differ significantly from those earlier excavations because they would be done in a systematic way, and in the process they would raise the standards of archaeology itself.

It was entirely by chance that Hallstatt first found its way onto the archaeologist's map. Set on the shores of the lake of the same name, the picturesque village of Hallstatt is located in northern Austria in the shadow of the Salzberg, a towering mountain with a heart of rock salt. For centuries, beginning around the year 1000 BC and continuing at least until the fourth century BC, when a landslide occurred, this mountain had been mined for its salt, a resource so precious to prehistoric peoples—both as a means of preserving food and as a trading commodity—that it has sometimes been referred to as white gold.

More than 2,000 years later, in 1846, salt was again being mined at Hallstatt when Georg Ramsauer, the mine's government-appointed director and the prolific father of 24 children, began excavating gravel needed to pave a road. To his amazement, he uncovered a human skull and a bronze earring. Curious, he continued to dig and slowly unearthed a complete skeleton. After removing a few more shovelfuls he found the remains of a second body, wearing the bronze bracelet that had circled its wrist on the day it was buried.

Ramsauer had a hunch that the two burials might be part of an ancient cemetery and set out to test his theory. Carefully staking out a four-square-yard area, he slowly skimmed away the topsoil. One skeleton came into view, then another, and still more. By the time he had removed all of the topsoil from his test plot, Ramsauer had unearthed a total of seven skeletons, the remains neatly arranged in two rows. Most of the bodies were adorned with bronze jewelry that, Ramsauer was convinced, was the work of "heathens." Eventually, the approach of winter left Ramsauer with no choice but to replace the soil and to put off any further excavations until spring. Ever the dutiful civil servant, he did, however, report the find to his superiors in the Austrian government.

Eventually, word of Ramsauer's find made its way to the Imperial Cabinet of Coins and Antiquities. Heading this bureau was Baron von Sacken, who immediately recognized the discovery for the opportunity it presented. Eager to add to his government's collection of antiquities, especially when these particular antiquities promised to predate those already in the collection, von Sacken encouraged Ramsauer to resume his excavations in the spring and provided the young mine director with funds and detailed instructions for conducting the dig.

May 1847 found Ramsauer back in his "heathen" cemetery. Little could he imagine then, as his workers began turning over the soil, that he would devote the next 17 years of his life and much of his own money to the ensuing excavations. Nor could he foresee that by the time his men finally put down their shovels he would have unearthed a total of 980 graves, recovered more than 6,000 bronze, iron, and gold artifacts—jewelry, pottery, tools, weapons, and great bronze cauldrons, as well as bits of clothing—and added immeasurably to the understanding of European prehistory.

It was fortunate that Baron von Sacken chose Ramsauer to excavate the Hallstatt cemetery, since there was probably no man more suited to the task than the conscientious and methodical director of the Hallstatt salt mines. Following the baron's precise instructions, Ramsauer carefully documented every stage of his excavations in a diary, kept a running inventory of all the recovered artifacts, and frequently sup-

Scene of the greatest early discoveries of Iron Age remains, the 800 BC Hallstatt cemetery lies in the clearing halfway up Austria's towering Salzberg—or "salt mountain"—in the right of this photograph. Because of the revealing finds made there by Georg Ramsauer (inset), the name Hallstatt came to apply to the entire early period of Celtic culture. The modern village of Hallstatt, a modest resort, is on the lakeshore at the foot of the mountain.

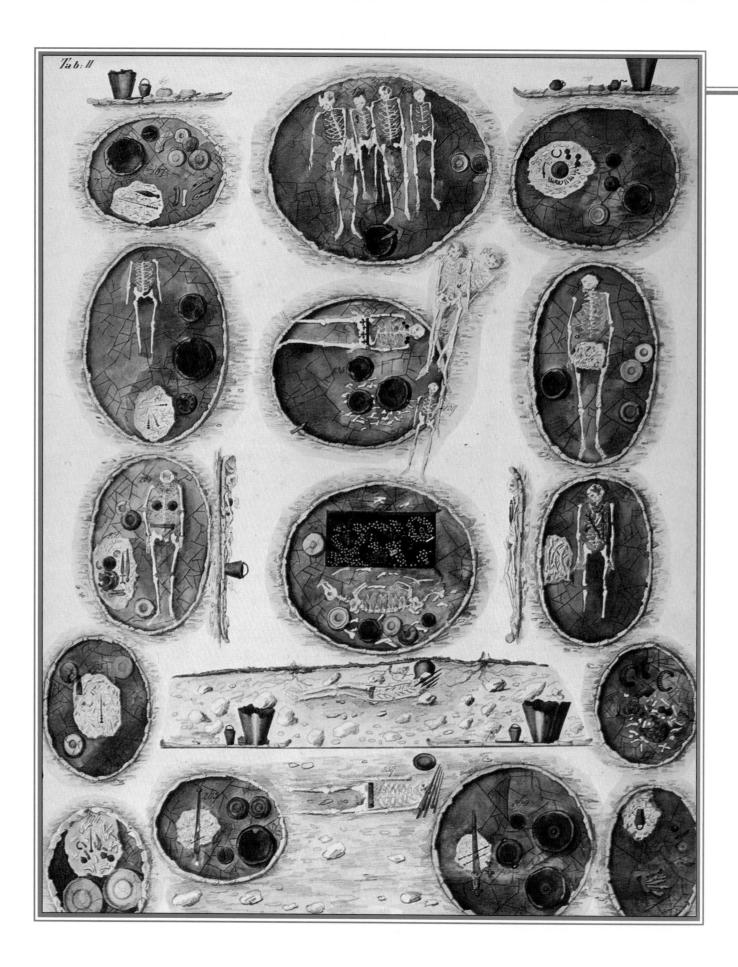

plemented those records with watercolor drawings he had commissioned of the actual graves and their contents. He was less diligent, however, when it came to the disposal of the artifacts: While the government took its share, many items were simply given away with no record of their subsequent whereabouts. Ramsauer's diary has since disappeared, although other documents he wrote after completing the excavations are still available.

In the Hallstatt cemetery the Bronze to Iron Age transition was visually demonstrated in a striking manner, as scholars discovered iron weapons and the identical weapons of bronze that they had replaced. Moreover, some 45 percent of the burials were cremations, while the rest represented the shift to inhumation. In regions to the north, Hallstatt-style brooches and pottery of the same period were found with bronze weapons only, affording evidence that iron had spread from south to north. The earliest ironworks at Hallstatt probably sprang up around 1000 BC, as the new metalworking techniques arrived from the south. It was this fundamental advance in technology that helped spur the spread of the Hallstatt culture across Europe and into the British Isles.

Given the variety and volume of the artifacts recovered at Hallstatt, as well as the similarity between these finds and those unearthed at other Celtic sites dating from the same period, it was only logical that the Hallstatt cemetery should become synonymous with the dominant culture of early Iron Age Europe. There was no immediate recognition of the Hallstatt people as Celtic; indeed, that identification was only gradually made, as scholars studied the ramifications of this seminal Iron Age civilization.

Hallstatt artifacts displayed a new artistic mode that emphasized overall design rather than individual detail; over the course of nearly three centuries, the style became ever more sophisticated (page 30). By charting the chronology of this stylistic development and noting the sites where its various modifications appeared, scholars could trace the movement of Hallstatt culture west through France and north into Britain.

In its thrust outward, this new culture first gave rise to larger settlements, since the technological advances that can be seen at Hallstatt required greater numbers of workers. Even more-substantial communities, such as Hallstatt itself, were later established, where at

More than a dozen of the ancient graves discovered at Hallstatt, some drawn in side view or from above, appear in one of the detailed watercolors done by Ramsauer's artist colleague Isidor Engl. The meticulous Ramsauer was far ahead of his time in excavation techniques, carefully exposing the graves and cataloging their contents. Most contained everyday items—pots, bowls, implements—but a few, such as the one at center, yielded quantities of fine ornaments in bronze and gold.

EYES IN THE SKY TO SEE THE UNSEEN ON THE GROUND BELOW

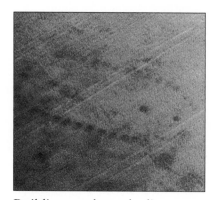

Building on the early discoveries of Georg Ramsauer and other 19th-century pioneers, archaeologists have produced an explosion of knowledge about the Celts—often with the aid of aerial cameras. Curiously, signs of ancient habitations that remain stubbornly invisible on the ground can often be seen with astonishing clarity from a thousand feet in the air. Outlines of long-buried foundations, ditches, earthworks, roadways, grave sites, and street plans of entire towns leap into focus when captured by high-flying lenses, even when the land has been inhabited, worked over, and plowed for hundreds of years.

The key to this phenomenon is the ability of the cameras to capture tiny variations in soil and vegetation that an earthbound survey could easily miss. From the air, buried walls still show telltale outlines in the subtly different color of the thinner soil above them or in the varied textures and color of the vegetation covering them. Patterns of plant growth also betray ancient ditches and postholes *(left, above)*, hidden roads and ramparts, among other things. This is because such depressions tend to retain moisture, making any vegetation in them taller and greener than that of the surrounding area. Aerial pictures taken in slanting light can catch shadows created by otherwise invisible mounds and hollows that may hide other remains of age-old settlements.

The pioneers of aerial archaeology started in the early 1900s with black-and-white film—which is still widely used for its ability to heighten contrasts. Since then scientists have added color film that picks up shifting hues in vegetation invisible in black and white and, more recently, infrared photography that, among other things, detects sources of heat such as ancient masonry. On the frontier: pictures taken from satellites that cover huge stretches of territory, revealing to practiced eyes such things as the buried paths of ancient trade routes snaking across the land for hundreds of miles or cities hidden under shifting sands.

Taken in 1976 during a drought, the aerial photo (above) *of a field in the Oise part of France clearly reveals a series of ancient postholes in the dry gound cover. Alerted by the telltale pattern of holes, archaeologists excavated the site, finding the remains of a Celtic dwelling built 2,000 years ago, which can be seen in a second aerial photograph at right.*

any one time anywhere from 150 to 300 people may have lived. Many of these larger towns lay along trade routes or, like Hallstatt, were sited near deposits of salt, iron, copper, or tin.

Trade was the source of Hallstatt's prosperity, as revealed by the numerous foreign imports Ramsauer unearthed in its cemetery. Among many other items were amber necklaces from the Baltic region, ivory sword hilts from Africa, bronze wine flagons and cauldrons from Greece and Etruscan Italy, and bronze brooches, helmets, and armor from Slovenia. These were not only a measure of the buying power of salt, but also telling evidence of the town's wide-ranging commercial contacts. That so much of value had found its way into the Hallstatt cemetery is attributable partly to Celtic beliefs about the afterlife—that it was not some idyllic heaven or fiery hell, but a parallel world where one's earthly possessions would be every bit as useful as they had been on earth.

Graves in the Hallstatt cemetery were not equally endowed, however, suggesting some social stratification, perhaps a lower working class controlled by a warrior aristocracy. The disparity between the haves and the have-nots was even more apparent at other burial sites, especially those established after 600 BC, in the later Hallstatt period. By that time the profits from trade had given rise to an elite class of merchant princes or chieftains who resided in hilltop forts and in death took to the grave with them gold, pottery, and numerous foreign imports. The most opulent burials contained four-wheeled wagons on which the deceased was laid, together with a full range of harness fittings and other gear.

Entombment with the Celtic equivalent of the royal limousine was still the order of the day as the curtain came down on the Hallstatt culture in the middle of the fifth century BC. Simpler burials would again be the rule for the next 300 years or so. Then the pendulum would swing back as people gathered once more into fortified settlements, called *oppida*. Cremations would make a slow comeback. Jewelry, weapons, and ornaments throughout this period would display an entirely new and distinctive art style.

That style, like the culture associated with it, is called La Tène, and like its Hallstatt predecessor it owes its name to a single archaeological site. Moreover, like Georg Ramsauer's cemetery, that site owes its discovery to one man: Friedrich Schwab.

In 1857 Schwab was the wealthy and appropriately portly scion of a Swiss burgher family as well as an amateur archaeologist of some local renown. With the resources to finance all of his own excavations and the inclination to keep all of his own discoveries, Schwab was dabbling in archaeology, prowling Switzerland's lakes in a specially designed boat that allowed for the close observation of the lake bottom and using a custom-made scoop to dredge antiquities from the drowned remains of ancient lake dwellings.

Exposed when the water level dropped in the late 19th century, rows of stubby posts litter the shore of Switzerland's Lake Neuchâtel near the ancient Celtic ritual-offering site called La Tène. Amateur archaeologists of the time concluded that the Celts used the timbers as supports for an ingenious offshore village built on platforms, as shown in the drawing at right done in the 1850s. Archaeologists now believe La Tène's Celts built their houses on dry land near the shore—but prudently propped them on stilts as protection against high water.

There were hundreds of these mysterious lake dwellings in Switzerland alone, some of them dating back to the Stone Age. Local fishermen had been snagging their lines for years on what some claimed were "submerged forests," but few in Switzerland's scholarly community had ever taken these claims seriously. Then, over the winter of 1853-1854, a drop in the water level of Lake Zurich left thousands of upright timbers protruding above the waterline, looking, lo and behold, just like the storied submerged forest. Stone axes, pottery, and tools made of stags' horns could also be seen in the mud of the lake bottom.

Switzerland's scientists took notice, foremost among them Ferdinand Keller, president and founder of the Antiquarian Association of Zurich. Keller visited the site, examined the artifacts, and announced, with all the conviction a man of his prestige could muster, that the piles had once supported platform huts that had been built over the open waters of Lake Zurich by Stone and Bronze Age peoples. In his enthusiasm for his own theory, Keller did not consider that the lake levels might have fluctuated over time, that the huts might have stood on what had once been the shores of the lake, and that the piles might have supported walls and roofs rather than the huts themselves. In fact, it would take another century for later generations of archaeologists to prove precisely those points.

Swiss lakes became trolling grounds for dozens of scientists, collectors, and treasure seekers, Friedrich Schwab among them. By 1857 the same prolonged drought that had caused Lake Zurich to re-

cede produced a similar effect on the waters of Lake Neuchâtel, eventually exposing rows of wooden piles along the eastern edge of the lake at a place known locally as La Tène, or "the Shallows."

Eager to add to the considerable number of lake dwellings he had already discovered, Friedrich Schwab sent one of his assistants, Hans Kopp, to La Tène to investigate. Once there, Kopp focused his efforts on a small area of the lake bed around a promising-looking mound of rocks not far from where the Thièle River enters the lake. Angling for artifacts with Schwab's long-handled scoop—demonstrating in the process why Schwab liked to call his assistants fishers—Kopp soon recovered the first of what quickly became a hoard of swords, scabbards, spearheads, and other weapons.

By the spring of the following year Schwab himself was on the scene, with a small fleet of his specialized boats. During the next three years he and his "fishers" dredged every square inch of the site. By 1860, when they hauled in their scoops for the last time, they had plucked hundreds of artifacts from the lake bed. Even then, thousands more remained buried in the mud. Many of these were recovered beginning in 1868, when the canalization of the Jura waterways lowered lake levels still further, allowing the archaeologist Emile Vouga, working with the Neuchâtel Museum, to excavate the site on dry land. Besides some 3,000 artifacts, he discovered the remains of buildings and two bridges that spanned a stream there, suggesting trading posts as well as a fortified settlement.

Schwab maintained that La Tène was just another pile village. Although this notion has been challenged, some scholars have continued to believe that La Tène was a Celtic settlement—perhaps even an industrial center—that, like other supposed lake dwellings, had been built on a lakeshore and later flooded when water levels rose. More recent research, however, supports earlier speculation that the timbers that had attracted Schwab's attention in 1857 were the remains of an Iron Age bridge that had spanned the Thièle River. According to this theory, beginning as early as the third century BC and continuing until the middle of the first century BC, La Tène had been an important cult site. Here, Celtic pilgrims crossing the bridge had tossed votive offerings into the water, probably to appease the spirits that were thought to animate the river. The discovery of a number of human skeletons suggests that human sacrifice may also have played a part in the religious observances at La Tène. This argument has been strengthened by a similar site consisting of the remnants of a bridge across the Thièle River at Cornaux, about two miles from La Tène, discovered in 1965 and dated to the late second century BC.

Except for the specter of human sacrifice, it is the ordinary artifacts extracted from the muck of La Tène that are so remarkable. So far the various excavations have yielded an extensive collection of extremely well preserved weapons and horse gear, tools, ornaments, coins, and other objects, including a complete wheel. Stirring the most interest among scholars were more than 160 swords, often with their scabbards, the long, slim profiles a sharp contrast to the short daggers of the late Hallstatt culture. The iron scabbards were chased with intricate designs that showed a marked departure from the simpler geometric patterns of the Hallstatt style. Spirals loop and tendrils swirl over La Tène scabbards, combining to create continuous patterns that convey an innovative sense of motion.

The originality of this artwork was not lost on the unflappable Ferdinand Keller who, after examining the La Tène swords, concluded—correctly this time—that they predated the Roman era and were the work of Iron Age Celts. Yet not everyone was so easily con-

Decorated with a complex set of patterns, the earthenware plate above from the seventh century BC shows the masterly handling of geometric designs achieved by Celtic artisans of the Hallstatt culture. The circular bronze harness plaque at right, with its intricate network of loops and swirls modeled after lotus flowers, belongs to the flamboyant curvilinear art of the later La Tène culture that flourished after about 500 BC. The plaque was found in a grave at Somme-Bionne in the Marne River valley of northern France.

vinced. In fact, in the years immediately following their discovery, the La Tène swords and scabbards were not considered Celtic in design, and certainly not in origin, by the majority of Keller's mid-19th-century contemporaries. These scholars often gave credit where credit was not due—to the Romans, to the Etruscans, or even to the Teutonic tribes of the north.

Recognition of La Tène as a distinct Celtic culture was, however, not long in coming. In the early 1860s, Napoleon III, anxious to prove a link between the pre-Roman Gauls and the French of his own time, ordered the excavation of the remains of a number of Roman camps in France. In a ditch near one of the camps, at Mont Réa in Burgundy, the royal excavators turned up swords bearing La Tène-style markings. Of greater significance was the fact that the swords were found in association with Roman coins, all dating to the period before 54 BC when the Romans marched into Gaul proper. They had probably been acquired through trade. As a result, archaeologists could reliably ascribe the La Tène style to the pre-Roman era in Gaul and could date these artifacts to the middle of the first century BC. Thereafter, the La Tène artistic style would be seen as the defining hallmark of the La Tène culture, which represented the apex of Celtic power and influence.

The discovery could not have been more timely. Elsewhere in Europe other La Tène-style artifacts were surfacing with increasing frequency, and scholars found themselves somewhat cautiously plotting the frontiers of the La Tène culture from Italy to Ireland, from Spain to the Ukraine. Convincing archaeological evidence of the spread of the Celts came in 1871, when French scholar Gabriel de Mortillet and his Swiss colleague Emile Desor pointed out the artistic similarity among the weapons and brooches found in a cemetery in the Etruscan city of Marzabotto, near Bologna; those recovered from Iron-Age graves in northeastern France; and others from

La Tène itself. The Celts, documented through historical writings as the invaders of Italy in the fourth century BC, finally had that reputation confirmed archaeologically.

A new conceptual framework was offered in 1872 when Swedish archaeologist Hans Hildebrand proposed a further division in Thomsen's three-age classification, splitting the Iron Age into two separate periods, the Hallstatt and the La Tène. This distinction enabled scholars to perceive these eras as two stages of Europe's Iron Age development. Accordingly, Hallstatt and La Tène came to lend their names not only to their respective art styles but also to the two major periods of Iron Age prehistory. The Hallstatt era bridged the late Bronze and early Iron Ages, lasting from about 800 BC until 450 BC, while La Tène Celts spanned the late Iron Age, from about 450 BC until the birth of Jesus.

Different segments of Celtic society evolved at separate paces, however. The late Hallstatt and early La Tène periods may have followed one another in some areas, while overlapping somewhat elsewhere; several Hallstatt settlements continued through the early La Tène period. Moreover, although in theory the La Tène culture ends with the subjugation of the Celts by the Romans in the first century AD, in reality the Celts lingered on in Ireland, which was never invaded by the Romans and thus never Romanized. In the late Iron Age the Emerald Isle provided a sanctuary for Celtic culture where, though modified by Christianity in the fifth century AD, many Celtic traditions survived. As a result of these discontinuities, most scholars today find it more useful to think of Hallstatt and La Tène as two decorative traditions as well as two periods of time.

Back in those heady days of prehistory, the Celts were a force to be reckoned with. To traverse Europe, from 500 BC onward, was to cross a largely Celtic continent. And to encounter the Celts was to meet a people that were on the rise.

A DUCHESS IN THE DIRT

Princess Marie of Windischgrätz hardly seemed destined to become an archaeologist. Born in 1856 and raised on her family's estates in Carniola, a province of what would become the Austro-Hungarian empire, she was married young to a German cousin, Duke Paul Friedrich of Mecklenburg-Schwerin. As the duchess of Mecklenburg, she embarked on a series of financial extravagances that led to her banishment to a castle in her native province, where, according to a contemporary, "she was forgotten by a world of which she was most fond."

Back home in Carniola, the duchess found an outlet for herself. Archaeologists had long been drawn by the region's many burial mounds and their rich troves of relics. In 1905 these seekers were joined by the duchess; trowel in hand, she soon became a familiar fixture at digs *(above)*.

No mere dabbler, the duchess—aided by her faithful secretary, Gustav Goldberg—kept meticulous records of her finds. She earned the respect of some of the most prominent archaeologists of the day, one of whom praised her for conducting her digs "in a truly scientific fashion." Her patrons included her cousins Kaiser Wilhelm II of Germany—an amateur archaeologist—and Emperor Franz Josef of Austria-Hungary.

Indeed, so passionately did the duchess throw herself into archaeology that she spent what was left of her personal fortune on excavations. And her efforts paid off, yielding one of the world's most important assemblages of Iron Age grave goods—more than 20,000 artifacts. Yet for all its worth, the collection would suffer some strange vicissitudes before finding a final home. The American gallery that kept the bulk of it for auction even considered tossing out the objects when sales failed to materialize.

ONE AMONG MANY: A RICH WOMAN'S GRAVE AT MAGDALENSKA GORA

The duchess undertook one of her most extensive excavations at a complex of burial mounds at a site known as Magdalenska gora, in present-day Slovenia. Among the 355 graves she uncovered was that of a woman—buried around 600 BC—whose grave goods suggest she was considerably wealthy. One intriguing find: a tiny arm ring, appearing at bottom right of the sketch below, that led to speculation that a child may also have been interred in the grave, although its small bones left no trace.

With the outbreak of World War I in 1914, the duchess ceased her excavations. The dissolution of the Austro-Hungarian empire after the war left her too poor to resume her work. In 1933, four years after her death, her daughter Marie Antoinette decided to sell the collection and shipped it to Switzerland. There, the scholar Adolf Mahr assembled a team of experts to examine the items in preparation for auction in New York. Guided by the original records, they indexed all available information about some of the 1,000 graves the duchess had opened, and photographed many of the objects. Out of their labors came a magnificent sales catalog, today considered a classic of its time.

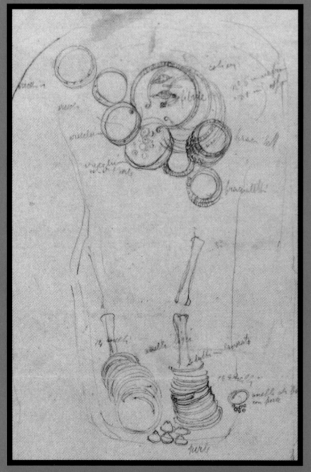

A sketch from the dig at Magdalenska gora shows the bones and artifacts as found in a wealthy woman's grave. Without this drawing, later researchers might have mistaken the clusters of anklets for bracelets.

Using the rough drawing at left as a guide, the grave's actual contents, including the skull and all the remaining bones, were artfully arranged and photographed in the laboratory of scholar Adolf Mahr.

These five bronze necklets from the rich woman's grave may have been worn together only on festive or ceremonial occasions. Perhaps as a grand and final gesture, indicative of the wearer's wealth and power, they were ostentatiously included in her grave.

A PAIR OF WARRIORS ENTOMBED
WITH FOUR OF THEIR STEEDS

Of all the hundreds of graves that the duchess excavated at Magdalenska gora, none was richer than the so-called warriors' tomb. Indeed, when Adolf Mahr and his expert associates cataloged the duchess's finds in preparation for auction, they deemed this grave's contents to be among the "finest and most interesting" in the entire Mecklenburg Collection.

Luckily, the duchess's ever-present secretary, Gustav Goldberg, had kept exceptionally detailed records of the dig. Two men had been buried in the tomb, which is thought to date from between 400 and 300 BC. Their bones had disintegrated with the passing of time, but the bronze helmets and an iron sword and spearheads found nearby spoke eloquently of their calling as men-at-arms. And the designs on some of their accessories testified to the skill of Iron Age artisans.

Buried with the warriors were four horses, two found with skeletons so intact that researchers have been able to determine that both were mature stallions, one about nine years old, the other much older. Interestingly, all of the horses were substantially larger than the small native variety commonly used in central Europe at the time, and thus had probably originated in Scythia, far to the east where fast-riding nomads employed such mounts. The steeds' iron and bronze trappings, too, were of Scythian design, further evidence of active trade between the two regions.

Remarkably complete after being buried more than 2,000 years, the skeleton of a Scythian stallion lies as it was uncovered during the excavation of the warriors' tomb at the Magdalenska gora burial mounds. Alongside the bones are a pair of two-handled bronze cauldrons, one plain and the other decorated at the rim and sides.

This bronze belt plate, graced with four figures of running and leaping deerlike animals, was attached to the ends of a leather belt. At the plate's left center is a riveted patch applied in antiquity to repair a crack.

Visible at the front of this well-preserved bronze helmet is a protruding rivet for attaching a flowing plume. Intended for use in actual combat, the helmet was fitted for a chin strap and for a caplike leather liner to reduce the pressure of hard metal on the wearer's head.

THE BRONZE CUIRASS OF STICNA:
ARMOR FIT FOR A KAISER

"Dearest Cousin: Please accept my sincerest thanks for your splendid gift! Goldberg arrived safely here with the treasure. Treasure it is and quite unique." Thus did Kaiser Wilhelm II, ruler of the German empire, begin a profuse letter of gratitude to his kinswoman the duchess of Mecklenburg in June 1913. Not long before, the duchess had dispatched to her imperial cousin several bronze spearpoints and an exquisite bronze cuirass—a set of upper-body armor—that she had unearthed at Sticna, not far from Magdalenska gora. And the appreciative monarch did not limit his gratitude to mere words: In the same letter, he disclosed that he had instructed his private secretary to deposit 100,000 German marks in the duchess's bank account. Per-haps mindful of her spendthrift ways, he stressed that these funds were to be used only for archaeo-logical work, and not "for any other purpose!"

Nothing that the duchess found in all her exca-vations can match the bronze cuirass for rarity and beauty. But the cuirass is not a part of today's Mecklenburg Collection at Harvard's Peabody Museum of Archaeology and Ethnology. Present-ed by the kaiser to a Berlin museum, it was seized along with many other items by the Soviets after World War II. It was restored to East Germany in the 1970s but languished in a crate in Leipzig un-til after the fall of the Berlin Wall in 1990. The cuirass was then returned to Berlin and is now on display at the city's Ethnological Museum.

Shovels at the ready, a brigade of locally recruited work-ers takes a pause during a day of digging at a burial mound at Sticna. The dark-jacketed man standing on the mound at top left is thought to be the duchess's secretary, Gustav Goldberg, who delivered the bronze cuirass found there to the palace of her cousin the kaiser.

The duchess of Mecklenburg, hat clamped firmly on her head and wearing a smock to protect her clothes from the dirt, kneels to free the cuirass from the earth. In thanking her for presenting the piece to him, the kaiser wrote appreciatively, "I stand up for archaeology!"

Its bronze still agleam, the cuirass was photographed at the Berlin museum where it has been housed since 1992, after being returned along with some 44,000 other museum pieces plundered by the Soviets at the end of World War II. The kaiser had it displayed in a glass case in his antechamber, where, he told the duchess, it was greatly admired by "savants."

FINDING AN AMERICAN HOME FOR ONE OF EUROPE'S GREATEST LEGACIES

In 1933, while on a visit to London, Hugh Hencken, curator of European archaeology at Harvard's Peabody Museum, was shown photographs of objects from the Mecklenburg Collection. Among them were artifacts that the duchess had unearthed at Vinica, site of a farming village that had flourished from about 300 BC until the start of the Christian era.

Unlike her digs at Magdalenska gora and Sticna, this one had produced little in the way of weaponry; rather, the 350 or so graves yielded a wealth of jewelry, much of it in the form of amulets and charms that were intended to ward off various dangers or promote good luck. "My eyes stood out on stalks when I viewed these pictures," Hencken recalled later.

The man who showed Hencken the photographs was the London agent for the exclusive New York gallery that the late duchess's daughter had chosen to sell the collection. Although, as Hencken wrote later, the gallery "dealt in art of the most costly kind," and its "auctions were black-tie occasions by invitation only," dealers backed away. To them, "these objects, mostly uncleaned and in the state in which they were found, represented nothing but rubbish." Since the Peabody lacked the funds to buy the collection on its own, Hencken tried to enlist other museums in a joint purchase arrangement. In that time of worldwide economic depression, however, no such partners could be found. Learning of this, the head of the gallery called off the auction.

Undeterred, Hencken negotiated directly with the agent for the duchess's daughter. In 1934 the agent sold him almost all the materials from Magdalenska gora, making up about 30 percent of the total collection. Five years later, the auction gallery went bankrupt and the balance of the collection was taken out of storage and put on the block. Hencken was the sole participant, and thus the Peabody Museum acquired the rest of the collection. Ironically, the duchess's daughter received none of the money, which was used to pay debts of the gallery when it went into receivership.

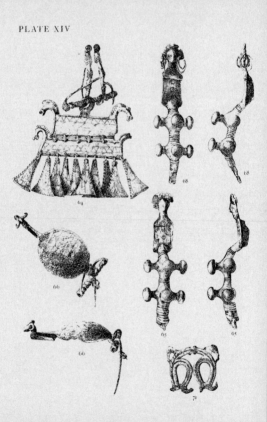

PLATE XIV

This page from the catalog prepared in 1934 for the aborted auction of the collection shows a selection of the charms and amulets that the duchess unearthed at Vinica, some seen in photographs on the opposite page. Because the material "transcends ordinary usage," the catalog bragged, "every endeavor" was made to preserve its scientific value, including leaving the artifacts in the state in which they were found.

Among the thousands of objects recovered at Vinica were these two human-headed fibulae, clasps used to hold the sides of a cloak together. The one at far left has a snake, thought to be of some religious significance, wriggling toward its head; the other head is framed by a semicircular halo.

Designed to be worn as a brooch, this bronze amulet originally featured four arched horses' heads, one on each corner; the head at the bottom right has broken off. The triangular pendants attached to the bottom of the brooch were intended to make noises as the wearer walked, apparently to frighten away evil or threatening forces.

A RISING TIDE OF POWER AND INFLUENCE

Part of German archaeologist Jörg Biel's job with the State Service of Antiquities of Baden-Württemberg was to follow up tips offered by local residents. So when schoolteacher Renate Liebfried phoned him in the spring of 1978, he readily agreed to meet her in the fields outside Hochdorf, a village some 12 miles northwest of Stuttgart. An amateur archaeologist, Liebfried had previously located several ancient sites in the vicinity. This time, however, Biel could see nothing significant in the mounds she showed him.

As he was about to leave, Liebfried casually suggested, "While you're here, you may as well look at the unusual rise in a field northeast of the village." She had heard reports that farmers' plows had been striking large stones.

Having seen similar sites, Biel knew, as soon as he glimpsed the swelling in the field, that he was looking at an Iron Age burial mound—and an imposing one at that. Some 197 feet in diameter, the tumulus—as subsequent investigation was to show—had once risen 33 feet. All but erased now by centuries of erosion and ploughing, its rounded form would have dominated the landscape for miles in the years immediately following its creation, proclaiming to all the power of a great Celtic chieftain.

Throughout the ensuing weeks Biel directed a team that cau-

Dating from the third century BC and found at a Celtic site in the Czech Republic, this abstract bronze animal head of La Tène design probably fitted over the neck of a wooden wine flagon.

tiously cut into the mound, seeking the burial chamber that he was certain lay at its heart. He wondered if he would find it emptied by robbers, as others in the area had been.

The big stones that had plagued the farmers also challenged the archaeologists working under Biel's direction. After a while team members began turning up bronze ornaments, largely pendants, possibly deposited at the mound as offerings by mourners. Anticipation grew among the excavators as they realized there was no evidence that anyone had broken into the tumulus.

Burrowing through layers of stone and decayed wood, the archaeologists gradually made their way into the remains of two structures—a large, rectangular, stone-filled space with a small room enclosed within it, undoubtedly the tomb itself. The archaeologists enthusiastically proceeded with the delicate work of clearing the rubble, secure in the knowledge that they were the first to enter the tomb in two and a half millennia. Later analysis of the fibulae—metal clasps used to fasten cloaks—found at the Hochdorf site would show that the burial dated from around 530 BC, the height of the Hallstatt period in central Europe.

Most of the contents of the chambers, including the skeleton of the man for whom the mound had been built, had been crushed or flattened by the fallen rock. The body discovered in the tomb had been laid out on a couch of burnished bronze held aloft by the raised arms of eight female figurines astride little wheels. The mound's noble occupant was tall, even by modern standards, and much of his six-foot frame had been decked with jewelry, from an astonishing gold torque around his neck to the strips of embossed gold that decorated his shoes. By his side lay a richly ornamented dagger in a gold sheath, while nearby were utilitarian iron objects such as a razor and nailclippers.

Numerous articles of splendor cluttered the room, including a large Greek cauldron for holding mead, a fermented, honey-based beverage. Fragments of the chieftain's clothing also survived, and these provided one of the excavation's great surprises. Among them were pieces delicately traced with embroidery and fastened with intricate brooches of twisted gold, remnants of a robe sewn of silk that had somehow made its way to Hochdorf from China.

The so-called Hochdorf prince represented, for Jörg Biel, "the find of a lifetime," and for Celtic studies its significance was tremendous. The community that could think of consigning such

Depicting a nude warrior, this life-sized sandstone statue from Hirschlanden, Germany, is of a type the Celts placed atop area burial mounds. He wears the customary torque, and his headgear is reminiscent of the birch-bark hat (page 75) found in the chieftain's tomb at Hochdorf.

wealth to the earth must surely have been wealthy itself. And it could not have grown rich without trading its own products far afield for commodities as precious as gold and silk.

As the Celts grew ever more affluent, powerful individuals within different tribes rose to the top both literally and figuratively. By the sixth century BC, Celtic warlords were perched astride a series of hilltop strongholds that dominated trade routes stretching from eastern France to southern Germany, western Hungary, and Bohemia. Some of these mighty chieftains may have started out as prosperous cattle dealers who eventually came to control the commercial passages. They were the aristocracy in what archaeologists have called a heroic society, one in which the fortunes and status of its leaders sprang from their fighting skills as well as their ability to recruit a loyal following. But in the end it would be these very attributes that would put communities at risk and would make them candidates for plundering by rival bands.

In a time of stability, when established trade routes satisfied most desires for goods and wealth, such raids were relatively few. When commerce was disrupted, as it was during the late Hallstatt period, young men ventured forth to replace with the spoils of war the wealth once achieved through barter. But as a loose collection of warlords and raiders, the Celts lacked a common goal and would never display enough political unity to form an empire, or even a nation, preferring instead to render their allegiance to individual tribes. Yet

This reconstruction of the Hochdorf burial mound is crowned with a statue, although no statue was found there. Had there been one, as is likely in the light of other finds, it was probably removed by early vandals. The actual tomb, protected by layers of stone, timber, and earth scooped up from the surrounding area, was located deep in the center of the tumulus. The faint rectangles in the right foreground show where workshops once stood. Items for the burial were probably produced here.

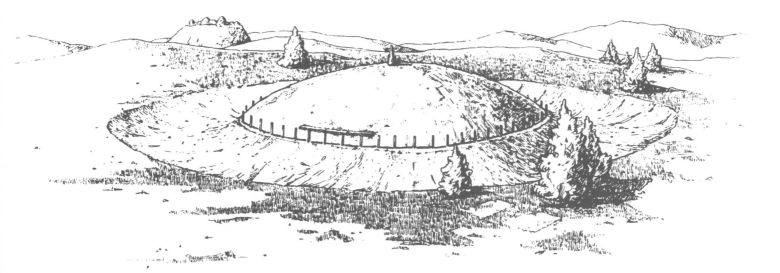

45

they would hold for centuries most of the terrain they settled, until Rome finally took control of their lands, assimilating much of the population and pressing the rest to the farthest margins of the west.

Because of the gold and costly goods recovered at Hochdorf and other Hallstatt interments, scholars have wondered whether such luxury items may have been included not merely to provide the dead with means for the afterlife but also to preserve the glowing names they had earned in life. A leader's final renown may have depended on the amount of riches that could be ostentatiously surrendered to the grave. In addition, the opulence of the burial may have bolstered the reputation of the deceased's brethren for allowing such wealth to be taken from the community and sealed away forever.

A similarly rich find had been made at Vix, in the Burgundy province of eastern France. There archaeologist René Joffroy had braved the storms of January 1953 to cut through the marshy, snow-covered earth of a largely flattened but 137-foot-wide tumulus that had once risen 18 feet high. His expectations were fully satisfied when he opened a ten-foot wood-paneled cube at the core of the mound to behold one of the Iron Age's distinguished dead lying on the platform of a four-wheeled wagon and laden with ornaments. Beautiful treasures were heaped upon and around the body in tribute to the rank and power of the grave's occupant, a woman. The most exquisite prize of all was a bronze krater weighing well over 400 pounds and standing about five feet tall *(page 49),* elaborately decorated and clearly the work of Greek—possibly Spartan—hands.

What was the source of such wealth? The sumptuousness of the sixth-century-BC grave is linked by some scholars with the tin trade. Vix marked the southernmost navigable point of the Seine River, where tin, used in the production of bronze throughout the Mediterranean world, may have been brought from British mines to be exchanged for luxury goods from warmer regions to the south. Large profits could accrue for those who controlled this busy junction. Some of the tomb's treasures, including the great krater, might have come from Greek merchants who sought access to the tin by making offerings to the local chieftain.

At Vix this ruler appears to have been a woman, some 35 years old. Joffroy believed and other scholars concur that in all probability the "princess

BIG STORIES TOLD BY TINY POLLEN GRAINS

The Celts did much to change Europe's environment when they chopped down forests to clear land for agriculture and to get wood for heating, smelting, and construction. Their impact can be measured through analysis of ancient pollen samples that reveal major shifts in vegetation patterns over time.

The walls of pollen grains are among the longest lasting of plant products; indeed, they are so resistant to decomposition, especially in the acidic and oxygenless conditions of peat bogs, that when samples containing pollen are placed in glass beakers and drenched with hydrochloric acid, the pollen survives while other organic material—even the beakers—dissolves.

Scientists can tell which plants the pollen grains came from. A preponderance of oak pollen in an ancient layer of peat suggests forest conditions; a decline in such pollen in the upper layers, marked by an increase in pollen from light-loving plants, often points to human intervention. European

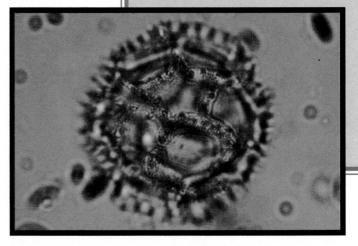

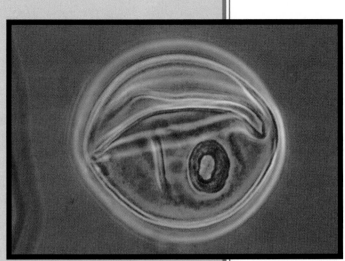

bogs, for example, showed an entire sequence, from the early, temporary clearing of some forest areas to the wholesale destruction of woodlands.

Sometimes pollen analysis produces surprises, as at Manching, Bavaria. For years, scientists thought thick stands of oaks had been cut to make room for this third-century-BC settlement. In the 1980s, however, pollen analyst Hansjorg Kuster discovered that the region had in fact been used as pastureland for hundreds of years. The pollen record revealed that oaks had gradually given way to pines and to grasses. Still, enough oaks had survived for residents to build a wall around their community. Heavily represented among the pollen grains were those of dandelion *(left)*, which thrives in open, sunny areas. Kuster also found abundant wheat pollen *(above)*, evidence that the inhabitants had grown their own grain.

of Vix" was not simply the wife or daughter of a prince but held power in her own right, possibly as a tribal leader. Her remarkable accumulation of riches, at the very least on a par with that found in other well-appointed graves, is cited as the most-telling evidence for this appraisal. Classical sources note the exceptional status of high-born Celtic women; "there is no rule of distinction to exclude the female line from the throne or the command of armies," the first-century-AD Roman historian Tacitus writes of the Celtic society he observed in Britain. A century earlier, Greek historian Diodorus Siculus commented that "Gallic women are not only equal to their husbands in stature, but they rival them in courage as well." At least three other Celtic burials from the Hallstatt period—one excavated earlier at Vix, the other two in central Europe—also turned out to be those of women, crammed with items indicative of their wealth and the high esteem in which the occupants had been held.

The graves of the aristocratic few contrast starkly with the burials of many others who took with them nothing more than ceramic vessels or a bracelet. Even these modest interments represent the wealthier members of a society whose poor apparently descended into oblivion. If the growth of trade and industry throughout the Celtic world produced fortunes, it also created vast social inequalities. In surroundings far less grand but no less fruitful than the Hochdorf and Vix tombs, archaeologists have traced the lives of less-privileged Celts and the economics that sustained the glory of this Iron Age culture.

Such a setting is provided high above the modern town of Hallstatt, tucked away in a gloomy ravine among high peaks *(page 22)*. To this day, salt is mined there as it has been continuously for several centuries. Throughout that time, local workers have been finding relics of their predecessors preserved in the encasing salt—bits of leather, wool, and linen clothing; pieces of pottery; and wooden dishes and spoons. As a matter of fact, in 1734 the intact body of an ancient miner was discovered, still dressed in fur and leather. He was probably a victim of one of the rockslides that make the area so hazardous. The men who had found the corpse gave it a respectful burial near the village church—although not, of course, in the consecrated ground reserved for good Christians. Beyond this, they

OUT OF THE MUD AND MUCK, GRAVE GOODS TO BEDAZZLE THE IMAGINATION

Few Celtic treasures discovered in Europe can match the rich finds that French archaeologist René Joffroy unearthed during his 1953 excavation of the so-called princess's tomb at Vix, located in eastern France. Sloshing through standing water that turned the archaeological site into a virtual quagmire, Joffroy and his team turned up an exquisite gold torque *(right)* and a huge bronze krater—used for mixing wine with water—that is the largest such vessel known to have survived from ancient times *(opposite)*.

Joffroy also found the princess's remains. Her skull was well enough preserved for a reconstruction of her features to have been carried out, as shown at left.

The round torque was at first taken for a diadem, since it was discovered close to the skull. Later study, however, indicated that the object had actually been designed to be worn as a necklet. And x-rays have revealed that the torque—made of pure gold and weighing just over 16 ounces—had been fabricated from about 20 segments artfully joined together. Some of these parts, such as the round balls at the ends of the torque, had been beaten out of thin sheets of metal, while others, such as the tiny winged horses at either end, had been cast using the lost-wax process.

The torque may well have been crafted by a local goldsmith. But the giant krater—standing five feet tall, it weighs

The princess's gold torque lies next to her skull, where it was found in the muddy tomb (above). *An end of the refurbished torque is shown at right.*

48

Archaeologist René Joffroy (far left) and a colleague prepare to remove the enormous bronze krater from the mire. The frieze surrounding the vessel's three-foot opening can be seen below.

some 450 pounds and was designed to hold nearly 250 gallons of liquid—almost certainly was made elsewhere, perhaps in Sparta or in a Greek colony in southern Italy.

The vessel may have been transported to its final destination in pieces and then put together. The decorative frieze circling the krater's neck, for example, is made up of 23 sections, on the back of which are Greek letters and other symbols corresponding to markings on the neck. Presumably, these notations were intended as guides to ensure that each section of the frieze was riveted in the correct position.

displayed relatively little curiosity about their distant predecessor.

Modern archaeologists have been far more attentive, working alongside miners to note any item of interest as it turns up. So far they have identified some 12,300 feet of prehistoric galleries, thrusting almost a mile into the hillside and plunging to a depth of nearly a thousand feet. And from the dimensions and length of the tunnels they have estimated that approximately two and a half million cubic yards of salt were extracted by the early miners. Conditions must have been abysmal. To protect their heads, the miners wore tasseled leather caps, rather like modern ski hats in design. Bone whistles for signaling in the narrow labyrinthine tunnels have been found, along with fragments of fir and spruce, used as torches to light the dark spaces underground.

Austrian geological engineer Othmar Schauberger has used replicas of Hallstatt tools to reconstruct the miners' working methods. At first the men would simply chip away at the unyielding crystal and scoop up the fallen slivers with wooden shovels. But a change took place around 800 BC when, judging by the high quality of many of the goods placed with the dead in the cemetery excavated by Georg Ramsauer in the 19th century, output seems to have reached its height and the town grew prosperous. A more efficient mode of extraction had developed, with men working in pairs. While one held his pick steady against the hard rock, his partner swung a wooden mallet, striking the pick on its head to send it biting into the salt. Moving the head carefully after each stroke to trace out a heart shape, the skillful worker could pry away solid blocks of salt weighing about 25 pounds each. Porters stooped under hide rucksacks, held rigid by wooden frames, as they carried the salt to the surface or to central collection points.

One such pickup depot was recently identified by Fritz Eckart Barth, a leading authority on the Hallstatt mine, who came to his discovery through a reference he chanced upon in a government report of 1748. Barth was intrigued by the mention of a proposed shaft extension that the mine administration had been forced to abandon when "remains of pine torches and other dirt" blocked its completion. He located the spot and found, in the "dirt," a rope of twisted bark fibers and a wooden pail with a capacity of more than 26 quarts. Salt had been brought here from the surrounding tunnels to be hauled or winched to the top through a vertical shaft. Here Barth also came upon leather mittens, used as protection for the hands of

Among the many Celtic artifacts uncovered in the Hallstatt salt mines are unused pine torches, gathered in a bundle and bound together with plaited linden-tree fibers (above, right), and a leather backpack, both dating from about 900 to 800 BC. The ancient miner slung the pack over one shoulder with the strap and balanced it over the other shoulder by holding the wooden handle seen above. When he entered the mine his pack would probably have been filled with torches to light his way; on the return trip it would have been loaded with salt.

the men raising and lowering the heavy bucket on its abrasive rope.

For archaeologists the Hallstatt mine has proven as rich a prize as any princely tomb, even if some of its treasures may seem unlikely ones. More than 100 pieces of fabric have been found and analyzed. While simple textiles of the basket-weave and cross-twill types predominate, there are more sophisticated materials in which threads of various colors have been woven into patterns. Cloth appears to have been cut to size and sewn into shaped, tailored garments.

Traces of cooking fires and utensils, including a spoon, ladle, and narrow-necked cooking jar, suggest that miners spent a great deal of time underground. Feces preserved in the salt have yielded clues to the miners' diet. A dedicated cook, Barth has managed to reconstruct from microscopic analysis of the evidence a gruel of the kind the miners might have eaten. He simmers chunks of lamb or pork with beans, barley, and millet and seasons the mixture with salt and such herbs as thyme and parsley, then serves it with chopped chives and onions. One of the spoons found in the mine still bore a crust of millet from just such an underground meal.

A community of people associated with the mines sprang up close to the tunnels. The inhabitants who would find their last resting place in the cemetery either worked underground, owned interests in the enterprise, organized the distribution of the salt, or defended the settlement from attack. Aside from fish caught in nearby lakes, food had to be imported from outside. Such a specialized center, buying what it needed with an economic surplus generated by its activity, was a novelty in a region whose population had hitherto lived largely in scattered, self-sufficient little agricultural communities.

Salt, which engendered the wealth at Hallstatt, was a necessary commodity used not only as a preservative of meat and fish, but also in the production of leather. Its commercial value can be judged from the amount of effort that had been involved in opening the mines. Schauberger estimates that, with the tools then available, reaching the salt through the rock would have required three to five years of labor.

The impressive scale of the Hallstatt undertaking and the long-term vision it implies represent a considerable departure from a tradition of peasant farming. Yet complex enterprises of this sort were increasingly the norm in an age named for the metal that would eventually become the basis for its prosperity.

In this image on a pottery sherd from Celtic Britain, a local deity—probably modeled in part on Vulcan, the Roman god of fire—is shown wielding hammer and tongs and beating a piece of iron on an anvil. The forests that still covered much of Europe at the time provided the necessary fuel for smelting and forging the metal.

Iron, it is believed, was first produced in Asia Minor during the third millennium BC as an accidental by-product of copper or lead smelting and proved superior to bronze in durability and malleability. By 1300 BC, iron technology had become a closely guarded secret of the Hittites, inhabitants of Turkey's Anatolian region. When the Hittite empire began to disintegrate in the turmoil that gripped

Mediterranean and Aegean peoples at the end of the Bronze Age, the techniques of ironmaking spread to the world beyond.

Two iron pins found in a ninth-century-BC grave at Seddin, Germany, mark one of the early appearances of the metal in central Europe. At this stage it was a luxury import. Although its manufacture was soon taken up across Europe, where the ore occurred in different places, iron remained a precious commodity and did not fully replace bronze in general use for some centuries.

As ironworking know-how developed, the Celts learned to crush the ore, layer it with charcoal to lower iron's normal melting point of 3,004 degrees fahrenheit, and intensify the heat with the aid of bellows. Impurities melted away, leaving a "bloom," a black, spongy core of carburized iron—iron that has absorbed carbon—which the metalsmiths then placed on special hearths and beat. They then forged the metal into the desired shape through continued heating and more hammering. Eventually, the smiths developed a technique called fagoting, in which successive layers of iron—some more carburized and hence stronger than those with less carbon content—were sandwiched together, heated, and hammered into a flat slab, or fagot. The fagot was hammered in turn; the end result was a strong, hard piece of iron, suitable for shaping into such a heavy-duty tool as an axe. The very act of converting something as base as ore into strong gleaming metal that could be shaped into implements and weapons must have seemed magical to many people, and indeed, blacksmiths in Europe would be regarded as having some kind of occult powers well into the Middle Ages.

Once mastered, iron production transformed every area of Celtic economic life as the metal came into general use during the sixth and fifth centuries BC. Sharp axes leveled forests and brought great tracts of new land into cultivation. There were iron hoes for tending crops and iron sickles for harvesting them, and reaping knives for cutting reeds or hacking leafy branches off trees. Small iron hooks served to strip away the leaves and to split the branches into supple sticks that could be used in the construction of wattle-and-daub walls.

When wood plows were eventually tipped with iron, they allowed farmers to turn over the soil in efficient furrows and to put into production ever larger areas, including ones they had previously been

Wrapped in a leather apron and buried, apparently by the smith who owned them, these perfectly preserved, well-made iron tools—including the anvil and hammerhead below—turned up in Austria. They date from between the fourth and third centuries BC. The owner may have been trying to hide his equipment from enemies, but something prevented him from returning for it; perhaps he was killed or captured.

Uncovered in England in 1984, this chariot burial from the first century BC bespeaks the marauding spirit of the Celts. The warrior, bearing seven spears and an iron sword, lay on the vehicle's iron-rimmed wheels; a cavity left by the disintegrated wheel at left has been filled with polyurethane foam to preserve its shape.

unable to work. In time, the countryside, cleared of its trees, began to take on the familiar patchwork pattern of many of today's cultivated rural areas as farmers removed stones from the fields and piled them up along the boundaries, where hedges sprang up. Hammers, chisels, drills, files, and nails became available for construction, advancing the carpenter's craft and improving living and working conditions, while iron knives, pots, and roasting spits facilitated more-efficient food preparation. So much did form fit function early on that modern hand tools are little different in their design from many of the implements used in the first century BC.

In a major breakthrough, Celtic smiths learned how to produce iron tires. They made them slightly smaller than the wheels, knowing that when the tires were reheated they would expand and could be slipped over the wood. As the metal burned itself into place and cooled, it also shrank around the wood, forming a tight fit. Such wheels rendered heavy-duty wagons sturdier still, thus increasing their usefulness—as well as Celtic mobility. (Interestingly, the word "car" derives from the Celtic root for wheeled vehicle, *carbanto-*, which is also the source of the noun "carpenter.")

Further refinements in tire production led to the evolution of the Celtic chariot as an offensive weapon that was light in weight, yet strong and maneuverable, and brought many victories on the battlefield. Thanks to the technological strides of the blacksmiths and wheelwrights, the Celtic iron-and-wood, spoked wheel would not change significantly until the 20th century and the introduction of the automobile. It is significant, perhaps, that the Celts represented the radiant sun as a wheel and often used the symbol in their art.

Iron ensured that personal weapons would become ever more lethal. No wonder Pliny the Elder called the metal "the best and worst part of the apparatus of life." The discovery of the iron-to-steel welding process enabled sword makers to take a great leap forward as blacksmiths learned that when the carbon content of iron is increased, steel is created. The technique made the blade harder and less prone to bend and snap, but it involved great proficiency on the part of the smith, with different temperatures required for the wrought iron and steel to be joined. The resulting steel edge rendered Celtic swords fearful slashing instruments. One Irish tale tells how the warrior Cuchulain dealt his enemy "a blow on the crown of his head which split him to the navel. He gave him a second blow crosswise so that three sections into which his body was cut fell at one and the same time to the ground." As a weapon of choice, the sharp-edged Celtic sword would survive, however modified, well into the feudal age.

Iron spearheads wreaked a particularly gruesome havoc of their own. According to Diodorus Siculus, they were longer than the swords. "Some are forged with a straight head," he wrote, "while some are spiral with breaks throughout their entire length so that the blow not only cuts but also tears the flesh, and the recovery of the spear tears open the wound."

As skills and demands grew, a wide range of new tools opened up possibilities for increasingly specialized workers such as armorers, wagon makers, and shipbuilders. Improved hammers, anvils, tongs, and rivets allowed the craft of ironworking itself to become more sophisticated. Soon artisans and traders began living and working in settlements where they could carry on their businesses in relative security and have ready access to customers. All told, by La Tène times, more than 90 kinds of artifacts were being manufactured from iron by Celtic metalworkers, and some were even being exported to the Mediterranean world, including North Africa. When European ironworking went into decline in the early part of the first millennium because of various upheavals, the craft would not again come into its own until between the sixth and ninth centuries.

Atop a steep bluff on the fringe of the Swabian Alps in southern Germany, the ruins of a citadel known as Heuneburg towers above the upper Danube. It was a stronghold of the Franks against the press of Hungarian marauders from the seventh to the tenth centuries AD, but actually its history reaches much further back than this—to Celtic times and the Hallstatt period. Eleven enormous burial mounds dating from the seventh and sixth centuries BC surround the citadel, and they attracted the attention of Eduard Paulus, the state archaeologist for the area, who in 1876 dug into three of the mounds and uncovered bronze vessels and gold jewelry. But it was not until 1950 that a systematic examination of Heuneburg commenced under the direction of Kurt Bittel, professor of prehistory at the University of Tübingen. Carving a trench through the ground to establish a stratigraphic sequence—the different layers of debris left behind by successive generations of inhabitants—Bittel tracked the settlement to 1500 BC.

Bittel's excavation of Heuneburg would provide a glimpse of

REINVENTING THE WAR CHARIOT

Hurling spears from their speeding two-wheeled chariots and then dismounting to thrust and slash with iron swords, Celtic warriors struck fear into the hearts of even their most battle-hardened enemies. But while countless spear points and sword blades remain to give a clear picture of the Celts' weaponry, no intact wooden chariots have ever been discovered. Scientists' estimates of the vehicles' construction and appearance have been based primarily on surviving metal parts and on depictions on coins and sculpture.

In the late 1980s Andres Furger-Gunti of the Swiss National Museum in Zurich determined to go beyond armchair conjecture and build a full-size working replica of a Celtic war chariot. To do the actual work, he hired an octogenarian cartwright who had, in his younger days, built a number of carts with wooden axles.

The cartwright was guided by various portrayals and descriptions of the ancient vehicles. In addition, he could refer to the museum's collection of bronze and iron chariot parts dating to the second century BC and to a pair of plaster casts, made in the last century, of a carved wooden yoke and a well-

preserved chariot wheel.

Using elm for the wheel hubs and ash for the rest of the pieces, the cartwright at last produced the chariot shown above. Each sturdy wheel is fitted with an iron tire; the open platform has the simple suspension system that archaeological evidence indicates was employed by the Celts. The platform and its occupants are protected from getting caught in the wheels by side screens made of steam-bent wood—as suggested by the image of a chariot with just such a device, depicted on an old coin.

In field tests over furrowed ground, Furger-Gunti found that his chariot was fully functional, and despite its shaking, he could hurl a spear from its moving platform just like a Celtic warrior of old.

commercial life in a typical Hallstatt-period hill fort. His most exciting discoveries belonged to a brief, bustling spell between 700 and 450 BC, a time of intense economic activity and political turbulence, when the site was home to a community of early Iron Age traders and artisans. The defensive walls girdling the citadel had been demolished and rebuilt more than 12 times during this 250-year period, while the settlement itself had been razed and reconstructed twice as often, which suggests just how chaotic and violent the times must have been.

In 1963 Egon Gersbach, who was serving as field director of the excavation, moved the painstaking work a giant step forward. Gersbach cut a section inward from the perimeter of the Iron Age settlement into the heart of the old living and working area. Here he unearthed remains of a collection of buildings skillfully constructed of oak and other timbers and clustered tightly around a central space. The inhabitants had dug an extensive system of ditches to drain one waterlogged section and then built rectangular wooden dwellings for as many as 300 people on the site. Gersbach uncovered workshops, complete with portions of their furnaces and chimneys. Bits of bronze, pieces of molds and clay crucibles, as well as slag from bronze and iron production indicated that the shops had been used for smelting and casting.

In addition to bracelets, necklaces, and small pins of bronze, Gersbach extracted from the Heuneburg earth more than 200 ornamental brooches, some, remarkably enough, inlaid with coral. The coral could only have come from the Mediterranean region and been obtained through trade. As the excavations and nearby graves demonstrated, the goods created in the Heuneburg metalworking areas were bartered for a range of foreign luxury products. Among these items was amber, from Baltic shores. The presence of numerous chicken bones pointed to a different kind of exotic import—the bird itself, brought north and bred here for eggs and meat.

Yet another delicious item—southern wine—made its way to

Heuneburg. The archaeologists uncovered hundreds of shards of Greek pottery that came from kraters used for mixing wine with water and spices, jugs for serving it, and drinking cups. Fragments of amphorae, the great ceramic jars in which wine was shipped, underscore the commercial importance of this beverage. The Celts themselves made only beer and mead, but their thirst for imported wine was to become a major source of profit for southern traders. "Many Italian merchants with their usual love of lucre look on the Gallic love of wine as their treasure trove," Diodorus Siculus wrote. He described how the much-desired product was transported both by boat on the rivers and by wagon through the plains. The price for the beverage was "incredibly large," he continued; "for one jar of wine they receive in return a slave."

Diodorus Siculus's fellow Greeks were themselves avid businessmen, as their founding, around 600 BC, of the trading city at Massilia (Marseilles) demonstrated. Celtic traders dealing with the Massilia merchants would journey down the mighty Rhone River, whose long valley, looping around the northern edge of the Alps, provided a convenient route. Shards of amphorae found at Massilia match perfectly those unearthed at Heuneburg.

More than wine and goods passed along such routes. The traffic in ideas and skills was probably at least as brisk. Countless shards of locally made pottery at Heuneburg suggest that Celtic potters attempted to capture some of the grace and symmetry of Greek and Etruscan works and to take advantage of new firing techniques developed in the south. But until the end of the sixth century BC the potters manipulated the clay by hand to form the shapes of foreign wheel-made pottery; only after the appropriate technology had

In this bas-relief from the south of France, burly workers wearing characteristic Celtic shirts and hair styles tow a heavily laden wine barge toward a port on the Durance River. Knowing of the Celts' enthusiasm for wine, Italian merchants carried on a lively commerce, exchanging wine for such commodities as iron, gold, and slaves.

worked its way north did they begin using the wheel. Several different types of Heuneburg-produced pottery have been discovered at the digs; much of it seems to have been mass made with outside customers in mind.

A major surprise of the Heuneburg excavations was the composition of the massive, bastioned wall that bordered the site to the north and south. In contrast to walls at other Celtic settlements, it was built of sun-dried clay-and-sand bricks bonded with straw, laid in a checkerboard pattern on a foundation of heavy stone blocks that had been hauled from a quarry about four miles away. A wooden walkway with raised sides and a series of watchtowers allowed guards to patrol the perimeter in safety. No wall like this has been found north of the Alps.

Plainly modeled on Greek examples—perhaps seen at Massilia—the Heuneburg brick wall is a remarkable achievement but not a particularly practical one. Quite unsuited to a damp, northern setting, in which the bricks crumbled, it compared unfavorably with the less showy earthen ramparts around it both in its effectiveness as a defense and in the amount of maintenance required. But the barricade was grand, southern, and modern; against the soft, tawny contours of the hillside setting, its bold lines, brought to dazzling sharpness by a coat of gleaming whitewash, must have announced to the world the booming prosperity and forward-looking enterprise of the proud community it protected.

All too soon this uncharacteristic rampart would become a blackened ruin. Its charred remains and the emptiness of the

Probably fashioned as an offering to a sea god, this gold boat model was found near an Irish beach. In vessels measuring about 100 feet long and 30 feet wide and equipped with a single square sail and eight pairs of oars, Celtic mariners plied coasts and navigable rivers. As seafaring traders, they extended Celtic influence throughout Europe and the British Isles.

stratigraphic sequence for a millennium afterward bear witness to the destruction of Heuneburg in the mysterious upheavals that, in the fifth century BC, brought the Hallstatt-period centers of industry to an end. Why so advanced a settlement as Heuneburg should have vanished is not clear. Unsettling shock waves might have resonated from farther east, where the warlike Scythian horsemen were bearing terror far beyond their native steppes, or even from the Middle East, where the collapse of the Assyrian empire had brought chaos and horror in its wake. But these events, if indeed they had any direct effect at all, would have caused mere ripples of disruption so far west, hardly sufficient to destroy a buoyant society.

What, then, happened? Some scholars believe that trade with the south was disrupted. The mounting tension between the Greek cities and their North African rival, Carthage, led, toward the end of the century, to a Carthaginian blockade of Greek shipping in the western Mediterranean. And the ensuing peace could only have made matters worse for the Celts, since it enabled the Greeks to establish new cities on the Adriatic coast at the mouth of the Po River and to open up the fertile plains and wooded Alpine foothills of northern Italy. Here, far closer to their home ports, Greek merchants could find all the materials they had previously bought from Celtic traders at Massilia.

Probably in large measure due to loss of trading opportunities, the economic basis of the Hallstatt civilization began to decline.

A conjectural view of the Celtic settlement of Heuneburg, Germany, includes the great brick wall, as it stood in the early sixth century BC (above). At the time, the eight-acre town was probably filled with dwellings and other structures; the drawing shows buildings only in those areas where foundations had been fully excavated by archaeologists. In the photograph at right, the wall's stone base and outer brick face are clearly visible—as are the charred remnants of a wooden walkway that was burned during an attack on the citadel.

Burials from the fifth century BC still show signs of wealth, but now they crop up in the countryside rather than around the sites of the commercial centers. The Greek connection seems to have ended, if the lack of Greek items in the graves is any indication. The foreign artifacts that have been recovered from these later graves tend to be Etruscan items intended for everyday use.

This upheaval in society produced dynamics of its own. Farmsteads still dotted the hills and plains, but enterprising young men now were looking elsewhere for reward. Some scholars find a symbol of the new era in the two-wheeled chariot, which starts turning up in warrior graves instead of the more customary burial wagon. As an instrument of war, the chariot bespeaks raiding, plundering, and the settling of conquered lands. The increased vigor of the times is also reflected in the appearance of the curvilinear La Tène style, which begins to grace Celtic weapons. Gradually the Celts of the La Tène era extended their influence from the central European homeland of the Hallstatt period north and west through Germany's Rhineland and France's Champagne region and beyond to Belgium and Britain. At the same time they thrust southward across the Alps, to burst upon the stage of classical history.

Grim and tired on a dark day around 391 BC, a dozen miles northeast of Rome, the consul M. Popilius Caenas addressed his assembled forces as he sent them off to battle. Roman troops had endured many rallying orations from politicians throughout the decades of conflict when their young republic was rising to a position of dominance among the states of central Italy. This time, however, they listened with concentration, for they knew the threat to Rome

was more ominous. "You are not facing a Latin or a Sabine foe who will become your ally when you have beaten him," declared the consul in the account given by the Roman historian Livy four centuries later; "we have drawn our swords against wild beasts whose blood we must shed or spill our own."

The next day the Celts must indeed have seemed like a pack of ferocious animals to the terrified Roman populace when they routed the army and went rampaging through the city in a spree of pillage and destruction. Settling down to besiege the last remaining military forces on the Capitoline Hill, the invaders would not leave the city until their numbers had been weakened by an outbreak of plague six months later. The cruelty and humiliation of the sack of Rome would burn into the consciousness of the classical world, strongly influencing attitudes toward the Celts. Some writers plainly regarded them as subhumans; others saw in them an admirable, untamed in-

In full battle array and accompanied by trumpeters (far right), *foot soldiers and cavalrymen advance into combat in this scene from a cauldron, dating from the second or first century BC, found at Gundestrup, Denmark. Just in front of the trumpeters is a soldier carrying a sword and wearing a helmet atop which sits a sculpted boar, a tusked, ferocious animal of the European forests.*

dependence of spirit that the more orderly, "civilized" societies of the south had lost.

The epic poetry of the Celts, as written down in Ireland centuries later during the Christian era, offers more nuanced insights into the "heroic" lifestyle of the aristocracy. Raiding the surrounding country from his hilltop stronghold, the warlord was—until a tougher, mightier rival appeared—ruler in his own locality. His authority derived not just from his wealth in livestock but also from the number and rank of the nobles he could command; their status in turn depended upon how many sworn followers—men bound to them by debt or by services rendered—they could bring with them into battle. These followers were heralds of the feudal societies to come. In fact, the term "vassal" derives from the Celtic word *gwas*, meaning servant or retainer.

War and conquest were woven into the Celtic economy. The agricultural labor of peasants might supply a subsistence for the ruling class, but it failed to provide the opulence the nobles required to prove themselves worthy. As during the Hallstatt period, revived trade helped fill the gap. And again, as in times past, plunder, kidnapping, ransom, tribute, and indemnities supplied further wealth and bolstered reputations. Status is important in every society, but for the Celts it was spelled out in explicit economic terms: According to later Irish laws, each warrior had a "man price," that is, the compensation that had to be paid if he was killed in a fight, as well as an "honor price," given if his honor had been destroyed. The Celtic view of a legal person included both his body and his honor or reputation. Not surprisingly, men of action in the upper ranks of society had higher man and honor prices than those beneath them.

There seems to have been an internal dynamic within Celtic society, evident especially during the La Tène era, that pushed its young men outward in a continual expansion: The chieftain was under constant pressure, since his strength depended on the number and loyalty of his warriors, who had to be bought with gifts of cattle and land to graze them on. If he did not provide these incentives, a rival would. Even the successful leader could not afford to rest on his laurels. His thwarted competitors would look beyond current frontiers to new territories where they might carve out their own areas of influence, spurring their men onward with visions of land and booty.

Always there would be fierce contention for wealth and power, and each successful warlord would in turn find himself threatened by a new generation of young pretenders. A convenient way for chieftains to deal with upstarts would have been to send the troublemakers away, letting them find their own horizons. If this was indeed the case, as seems likely, Celtic expansionism would thus have become self-perpetuating.

Ruthless and reckless, Celtic warriors struck terror into the hearts of those under assault. The very sound of a Celtic army in the field was enough to scare off many opponents. "They are given to wild outbursts and they fill the air with hideous songs and varied shouts," wrote Livy, who explained elsewhere that "their songs as they go into battle, their yells and leapings, and the dreadful noise of arms as they beat their shields in some ancestral custom—all this is done with one purpose, to terrify their enemies." As for their trumpets, Diodorus Siculus observed that they were "of a peculiar barbaric kind; they blow into them and produce a harsh sound that suits the tumult of war."

Celtic armor, as described by Diodorus Siculus, included individually decorated, man-sized shields. "Some of these have projecting bronze animals of fine workmanship that serve for defense as well as decoration." Bronze helmets to which were attached "large projecting figures," lent increased stature to the men who were already tall. Grave finds in the mid-Rhine and Champagne regions confirm Diodorus Siculus's account of the Celtic fighter's headgear but suggest that bronze or gold helmets were worn only by chieftains. The well-equipped Celt carried a shield, a number of spears, and an iron dagger and a sword, more useful for slashing than thrusting. Because such swords were unwieldy at close quarters, the enemy who held his ground stood at an advantage. This strategy was something the Romans would learn, to the detriment of the Celts.

Further commenting on the Celtic military during the La Tène period, Diodorus Siculus wrote that "they used chariots as the heroes of Greece are traditionally said to have done in the Trojan

The defiant bronze falcon poised atop this iron helmet from the third century BC menaces with outstretched wings that actually flapped in the motion of battle. Uncovered in the early 1960s at a chieftain's burial site in Rumania, the helmet and crest are strikingly similar to the headgear worn by some of the Celtic warriors in the depiction on page 62.

War." Their battle chariots, as indicated by remains in the richer graves, were light wooden vehicles with bronze fittings. They were built for speed and for show. A skilled charioteer usually drove, while behind him his lord strutted and threatened, alighting to engage the enemy hand to hand when the real fighting began.

The Roman general Julius Caesar, encountering chariot warfare in Britain in 55 BC, noted the disturbing effect of the wheeling, careening cars: "At first [the Celts] ride along the whole line and hurl javelins; the terror inspired by the horses and the noise of the wheels generally throws the enemy ranks into confusion." There was an air of showmanship about the chariot charge, an arrogance and a disdain for danger that would unnerve all but the most disciplined enemy forces. "Their daily training and practice have made them so expert that they can control their horses at full gallop on a steep incline and then check and turn them in a moment," Caesar reported. "They can run along the chariot pole, stand on the yoke and return again into the chariot very speedily."

Celtic warriors also resembled the legendary Homeric heroes in valuing individual glory above any wider battle plan. Irish sources confirm Diodorus Siculus's claim that "when the armies are drawn up in battle array [warriors] are wont to advance before the battleline and to challenge the bravest of their opponents to single combat, at the same time brandishing before them their arms so as to terrify their foe." Upon the acceptance of such a one-on-one fight by an opposing warrior, "they loudly recite the deeds of valor of their ancestors and proclaim their own valorous quality, at the same time abusing and making little of their opponent and generally attempting to rob him beforehand of his fighting spirit."

Shown against a stonework backdrop, these double-edged iron sword blades—their wooden handles long since decomposed—are characteristic of the weapons wielded by Celtic warriors in ferocious hand-to-hand combat during the La Tène period. At center, the smooth, unembellished bronze helmet with projecting neck guard is typical of the workaday helmets worn by ordinary soldiers. All of the equipment pictured dates from the third to first centuries BC and was recovered from two French rivers, the Doubs and Saône.

The Celts differed from Homer's warriors in at least one gruesome respect: "They cut off the heads of enemies slain in battle," reported Diodorus Siculus, "and attach them to the necks of their horses." This practice, noted by a number of authors, is also depicted in the sculpture of several classical monuments. Decapitation is alluded to as well in the Irish epics, and if any proof was needed of this grisly practice, archaeologists have found haunting evidence of it at a sanctuary discovered in Roquepertuse, France.

It is hardly surprising then that this people should have aroused such dread among their southern European neighbors, no mean warriors themselves. Nor is it strange that, despite the natural barrier offered by the Alps, such stalwart fighters should have been drawn to the soft, fertile lands that lay beyond the mountains, in Italy particularly. As Etruscan power declined, the Celts streamed across northern Italy, and by the middle of the fourth century BC they had made the region so much their own that the Romans were calling it Cisalpine Gaul, or "Gaul this side of the Alps," as opposed to Transalpine Gaul, or "Gaul across the Alps," the Roman designation for France. Meanwhile, exploratory forays by the Celts into areas as far south as Apulia, in Italy's heel, were causing grave concern in a Rome still scarred by the experience of 391 BC. As an ever-looming threat, the Celts would have a profound effect on the rise of Roman military power.

The Cisalpine Celts make their presence felt in Italy in two fairly conclusive ways: A new burial style and new settlement patterns suddenly appear in the archaeological record, a likely sign of some violent intervention from outside. Graves of the sort familiar from sites north of the Alps, containing iron weapons and ornaments in the La Tène style rather than the traditional bronze artifacts of the indigenous population, have been found.

The presence of weaponry in the Cisalpine graves implies the persistence of the aggressive Celtic heroic culture, yet a change seems to have occurred. While their incursions into the south may have begun as raids, many of the victorious Celts sent home for their families or married local women, settling down to a more peaceful existence as farmers.

Similarly furnished warrior graves dating from the fifth and fourth centuries BC have been found in the northern fringes of the Balkans. It was here, in 334 BC, that one Celtic war party came into contact with the forces of the young Macedonian ruler, Alexander,

Replacing the moldered originals, skulls stare from niches cut into the stone pillars of a Celtic shrine at Roquepertuse, in southern France. Like many ancient peoples, the Celts deemed the human head to contain the essence of a person's being, and they frequently lopped off those of prominent enemies defeated in battle and put them on ritual display.

on the banks of the Danube. Since Alexander the Great was on the threshold of his historic Asian adventure and the Celts had conquests of their own to pursue, the two sides signed a treaty of friendship and went their separate ways. Alexander's death in 323 BC left a power vacuum in Macedonia and thus in Greece as a whole. The Celts were not slow to take advantage of the resulting turmoil and to add to it by mounting raids deep into the Greek heartland.

In 279 BC, according to Diodorus Siculus and Pausanias, the second-century-AD Greek traveler and geographer, Celts sacked the religious center of Delphi, murdering the elderly priestess who presided over its famous shrine. Such sacrilege would have been regarded as an outrage, comparable to an attack on the Temple of Vesta in Rome. Greek reports of the Celts eating babies and drinking blood are surely untrue—they are identical to stories told about the Persian invaders of previous ages—but there can be no doubting the intensity and attendant horrors of the onslaught.

The Celts were still in Greece in 277 BC, serving as mercenaries to Antigonus Gonatas, one of a number of claimants to Alexander's succession in Macedonia and its empire. However proud they may have been, the Celts saw no shame in hiring out their services to local rulers in southern Europe. In 367 BC, according to the Greek historian Xenophon, the tyrant of Syracuse, Dionysius the Younger, paid Celtic mercenaries to support his Spartan allies in their conflict with Thebes. Dionysius would go on employing them for almost 30 years. At the same time, other Celtic soldiers of fortune were hiring themselves out to such powers as Sparta, Carthage, Syria, Egypt, and eventually even Rome. As a result of being paid in Greek-minted coins, Celts became familiar with money and soon began minting metal coins of their own, though this would not become widespread practice until the second and first centuries BC.

The loyalty of Celtic mercenaries was strictly to the highest bidder, and history records at least one occasion in which Celtic hirelings stomped off the job in a dispute over money. The price for their lack of discretion in choosing their clients was that Celts could find one another on opposite sides of the battle. During Hannibal's storied march through the Alps, for example, Celts in the employ of the Carthaginian army had to face the swords of other Celts defending their territory.

It was as mercenaries that the Celts entered Asia Minor in 278 BC. Warriors drawn from three tribes, the Tolostibogii, the Tectosages, and the Trocmi, presumably from somewhere in central Europe, arrived at the invitation of King Nicomedes of Bithynia, who wanted assistance in his struggle against neighboring despot Antiochus I. They brought with them their families and their way of life; after their service was over they built tribal hill forts, competing with one another as raiders and preying on farming peoples throughout the area. Eventually they would be more or less contained in a broad strip near modern Ankara that became known as Galatia. Besides the historical accounts of the havoc these newly settled Celts caused in this region, Galatia is primarily remembered as one of those communities later visited by Saint Paul, and pitifully few archaeological traces of their existence here have endured.

In 1960 researchers excavating a building in a fortified settlement at Magdalensberg, in southern Austria, stumbled upon a cellar that had lain undetected and undisturbed since it was abandoned 2,000 years earlier. The plaster walls were covered with several hundred inscriptions, the work apparently not of residents but of visiting Roman merchants. Handwriting samples by Romans of all periods have survived in such abundance that it is possible for experts to date any given piece of writing from the style of its script; in this case a date between 35 BC and 45 AD seems likely.

     Still clearly legible, the inscriptions provide merchants' names and home cities and list the goods they had bought. The traders had visited at all times of the year, and though most were from Rome, Bologna, and Aquileia, a Roman seaport at the head of the Adriatic, some had journeyed from as far afield as North Africa. Here at Magdalensberg, hundreds of anvils and axes changed hands, as did iron rings and clasps. Vessels such as jugs,

In 1986 this golden hoard of 386 Celtic coins was found by accident in a field in southern Germany. Dating to the second century BC, the coins had originally been buried in an iron container, but farmers' plows had scattered them over an area of several square yards. Coinage had been invented by the Lydians in the seventh century BC, but the Celts, having a well-established system of barter, did not start minting their own coins until about 400 years afterward.

basins, trays, and beakers of copper and brass were also sold in abundance. One individual, Sineros of Aquileia, had, for instance, bought 110 basins, weighing 15 pounds each. Three other merchants had arrived together; one left with 720 rings and 560 axes, a second with 550 rings and 510 axes, and the third with 560 rings and 565 axes.

As the cellar walls' list of goods would seem to indicate, five hundred years after the heyday of the Hallstatt culture in central Europe, the Celts were once again devoting much of their energy to commerce. Dozens of sites across the Celtic world had made the transition from raiders' hill forts into more advanced settlements that even the urbanized Romans would regard as oppida, or towns. Farmers from the surrounding countryside would bring their produce to the oppida for sale both to southern merchants and to the growing number of native artisans who manufactured iron and bronze goods for a living. Times were good. The perpetual military campaigning of the emerging Roman Empire had created insatiable demands for iron weaponry and armor, as well as for leather straps and harnesses. Romans wanted meat, cheese, honey, resin, textiles, and a range of other products that the Celtic peoples to the north could provide.

So much dependence on Roman markets, especially in Cisalpine Gaul, had the effect of making parts of the Celtic world, in economic terms at least, all but provinces of Rome. As the frontiers of the Roman Empire shifted northward during the second and first centuries BC and as Celts began to enter into increasingly lucrative commercial relationships with Rome, more and more Celts abandoned the countryside, attracted by the prospect of a better, safer life in the oppida. They did not forsake their fierce ways entirely, however: One of the most important commodities that these oppida provided Roman merchants was slaves, captured in neighboring districts by men who had not forgotten their raiding traditions. And beyond the immediate sphere of Roman influence, in regions to the west and to the north, the old ways persevered.

A TOMB BEYOND COMPARE

The ancient Celts who entombed their chieftain in a great mound near the modern village of Hochdorf, Germany, provided the dead leader with rich grave goods to accompany him into the afterworld. They also took care to guard the sumptuous burial chamber against graverobbers, enclosing it with plunder-proof layers of stone and oak timbers before heaping it over with earth. Thus, when the German archaeologist Jörg Biel excavated the mound in 1978 and 1979 he made that rarest of finds—an undisturbed Celtic grave dating to the early Iron Age, some 2,500 years ago.

But if the tomb had been spared from robbers, it had not escaped the ravages of time and nature. A few years after the burial and before the body had time to fully decompose, the 50-ton stone-and-timber roof collapsed into the chamber, reducing the mound's 30-foot profile to about five feet and battering much of its contents. At the same time, the mound's overly-

ing earth maintained a waterproof and airtight seal that, working together with copper oxides emitted by the bronze and copper artifacts, slowed bacterial decay and helped preserve much of the site's organic material.

The wreckage that filled the tomb presented Biel and his team with a major archaeological challenge. After erecting a sort of greenhouse over the site to protect it from the weather, they started to remove the cumbersome stone blocks. Soon they began to make a number of intriguing finds, not least among them a gold-adorned skeleton lying on the remnants of a large bronze burial bed supported by eight female figures on small wheels *(above)*. Other objects, painstakingly reconstructed and shown on the following pages, included a richly worked ornamental dagger, a conical birch-bark hat, a two-horse wagon, and a bronze cauldron. Not only do these reveal the uniqueness of the find, they also show what art restoration has become.

INSIDE A CELTIC BURIAL CHAMBER

As they carefully removed debris and plotted the location of every artifact in the Hochdorf burial chamber with the aid of a special mapping and drawing device, the German archaeologists could put together a detailed picture of the ancient tomb as it had appeared when sealed.

As shown in the drawing at right, the heavily reinforced walls and ceiling of the chamber, which measured about 16 by 14 feet, were draped with richly worked textiles; the planked floor was covered with coarser cloth. At the crypt's west wall

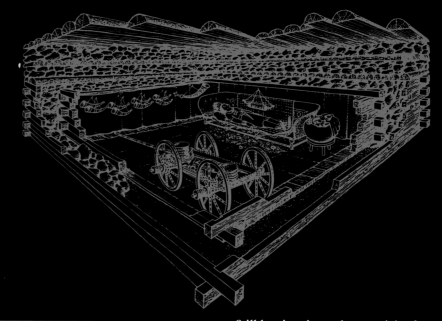

Still bearing the ponderous weight of a fallen roof timber (left), two of the eight bronze figurines supporting the Celtic chieftain's burial couch stand in the rubble that littered the tomb. They have little holes drilled in their chests, wrists, waists, and ankles filled with now discolored coral, suggestive of jewelry. The coral would have been obtained from southern traders.

Shown after extensive restoration, this one-of-a-kind Celtic couch was made of six riveted bronze sheets and embellished on the back with embossed depictions of wagons and sword dances. From fragments of material embedded in the seat, archaeologists determined that the couch had been thickly padded with various animal furs and woven hemp. Analysis of pollen from the funeral bouquets, caught in the bedding, indicated a late summer burial.

the chieftain's flower-bedecked corpse—amply cushioned with furs and cloth—reposed on a nine-foot-long bronze couch, shown reconstructed below, the only such item ever found at a Celtic burial site. Around his waist was a gold-covered belt. To equip him for an afterlife much like his life on earth, a gold-covered bronze dagger had been placed at the chieftain's side; within easy reach at the rear of the couch hung a leather quiver bristling with arrows tipped in bronze and iron. Covered with cloth, on which a gold

cup had been placed, a huge mead-filled bronze cauldron stood at the foot of the couch. Nine hefty drinking horns, one of them more than a yard long and made of gold-banded iron, hung on the southern wall.

In common with many Celtic graves of the late Hallstatt period, the Hochdorf tomb also held a four-wheeled, two-horse wagon. On the wagon bed lay a yoke and harnesses and some essentials for afterlife hunting and feasting: a spearhead, ax, and knife, along with three large serving bowls and nine plates.

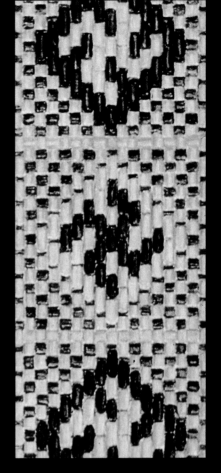

This drawing of a pattern found in a swatch of the cloth that draped the couch at the chieftain's head was re-created through microscopic study of fabrics found in the tomb. The swastika-like emblem crops up in many prehistoric cultures, but what significance it held for the Celts is unknown.

PROUD POSSESSIONS OF A CHIEFTAIN

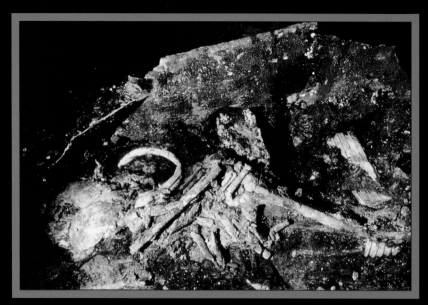

Examination of the skeleton lying on the burial couch *(left)* quickly revealed the exalted position that the dead man had occupied in life. His remains glistened with lavish golden ornaments, including an armlet and a torque. The tops, sides, and upturned toes of his leather shoes were decorated with strips of sheet gold; his intricately worked iron-and-bronze dagger was covered in ceremonial gold sheathing.

Among the most unusual finds was a flattened conical birch-bark hat that lay near the

Cleared of debris that had covered it, the chieftain's crushed skeleton lies on the remains of his burial couch. Just to the right of the neck is the gold torque symbolizing the wearer's earthly powers; at the center, one of the female figures that supported the couch pokes through a jumble of ribs.

chieftain's skull. Archaeologists had seen such headgear on statues, but did not know what they were made of until this example turned up. Like much of the tomb's fragile contents, the hat was removed by casting it in plaster along with surrounding objects; the resulting block was then taken to a laboratory, where the bark was delicately removed from the matrix and the hat meticulously reconstructed. All told, 18 such blocks were removed from the tomb.

Study of the skeleton revealed that the well-muscled chieftain had an unusually large head, stood six feet tall, and had been between 40 and 50 years of age. It also showed that he suffered from arthritis and had ground his teeth—perhaps because of his responsibilities.

A tribute to the restorer's art, the birch-bark hat is shown mounted on a plastic base that re-creates its original shape. It was sewn from two disks of bark and decorated with a "punch-line" design. Two holes in the brim accommodated a rough cord for securing the hat to the wearer's head.

The original gold sheathing covers a replica of the chieftain's bronze-and-iron dagger. It may have been made at the grave site. In the design below, taken from the back of the burial couch, Celts perform a sword ritual.

REBUILDING AN ORNAMENTED WAGON

One of the daunting jobs facing the Hochdorf archaeologists was restoration of the four-wheeled wagon. Buried under debris, its wood body almost entirely decomposed and its decorative sheets of iron fragmented, the wagon was little more than a gritty smudge on the floor *(right)*. Yet the restorers were able to fit the meticulously cleaned and chemically treated pieces back together over a newly constructed frame of balsa wood, aluminum, and synthetic resin *(below, right)*.

The restored wagon's shallow-

Surrounded by marking tags and the little boxes, bags, and foil used in handling fragile pieces, the remains of the Hochdorf wagon lie as they were found in the tomb. At the center, visible as a greenish clump, are the bronze bowls, dinner plates, and yoke and chain that once rested on the wagon bed.

Restorer Benno Urbon deftly wields an electric tool to remove corroded particles from a piece of an iron wagon wheel before affixing the fragment to the rebuilt wheel's plastic frame. The rims of the front wheels originally were made of ash and those of the rear wheels of elm, with elm and maple used for the spokes.

sided, rectangular bed is about five and a half feet long and a little over two feet wide. The iron-plated pole, or tongue, to which horses would have been yoked, protrudes more than seven feet to the front.

Most impressive of all, perhaps, are the enormous 10-spoked wheels. Measuring almost three feet in diameter, they feature large decorative hubs and are banded with heavy iron. Each of the four wheels took approximately six months to restore; missing pieces were replaced with plastic that blends with the original.

Wagons like this—or at least remnants of them—crop up in graves dating from the Bronze Age through the Viking era. They may have been intended to convey the dead into the afterworld, or they may have been nothing more than the hearses that transported them to the grave. The Hochdorf wagon is the most complete of all, thanks to the fact that so much of it was covered with metal fittings.

In this stylized depiction from the back of the chieftain's burial couch, a Celtic warrior wields a lance and shield while poised atop a wagon like the one found in the tomb. The scene gives a glimpse of the yoke used to hold the horses to the wagon pole (overleaf).

Extricated from beneath the bowls and plates on the disintegrated wagon bed, the maple-wood yoke was covered with a set of handsomely decorated bronze chains. Running in a line just below the yoke are rusted fragments of iron that once covered the wagon's wooden rim. To the far right, on the yoke itself, lies a little figure of a horse, part of its decoration.

Only this midsection of the worn yoke was intact, leaving restorers to guess about the placement of the bronze bands. The butter-soft wood had to be specially treated so that water could be extracted from the cells and replaced with a hardening wax.

Carefully restored to their original luster, the six Hochdorf yoke chains are anchored to a heavy ring that features a coral-encrusted conical disk in its center. The ring may have been strapped to the middle of the four-foot yoke, with some of the chains attached to the horses' bridles to hold their heads in place. The other chains may have been used to brace the standing driver.

79

A MEAD CONTAINER RESTORED TO GLORY

The enormous bronze cauldron standing at the foot of the chieftain's burial couch had once brimmed with mead, a heady fermented beverage made with honey. By the time Jörg Biel and his archaeological crew uncovered the tomb, all that remained of the mead was a brownish residue—which contained pollen from flowers that bloom late in summer.

After carefully removing the smashed cauldron, the restorers suspended the vessel on a pole and pieced the many fragments together on a backing of some 1,000 adhesive plasters made of carbon fibers and artificial resin, finally returning the vessel to its original appearance.

Cast in bronze, the cauldron stood 27 inches tall and measured 39 inches in diameter at its widest point. Interestingly, it held about 130 gallons, enough to fill the nine large drinking horns that hung on the south wall of the tomb.

Three cast-bronze lions were soldered with lead to the cauldron's rim, which was also fitted with three heavy-duty handles for hefting the bulky vessel. Unlike many of the items found in the tomb, the cauldron had not been made locally. Rather, it seems to have been fashioned in a Greek colony in the south of Italy and may have been presented to the chieftain as a gift.

Wielding an everyday vacuum cleaner, a restorer removes exterior dirt and debris from the remains of the cauldron for later examination (above). *Meanwhile, another technician applies* chemicals to harden the vessel's fragile walls before transport to the laboratory, where the cauldron was pieced back together* (below)—*an exacting job that took a year to complete.*

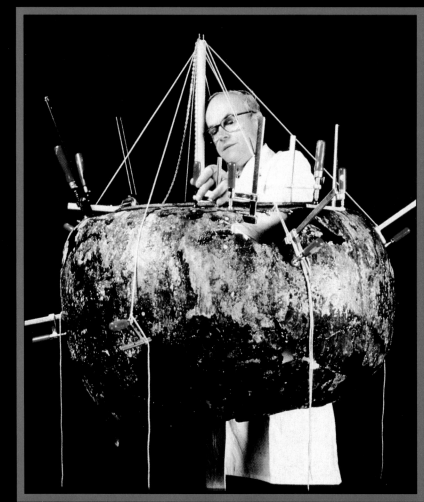

Hochdorf cauldron [...] when it was sealed [...] mb some 2,500 years [...] lion at right dif- *fered from the other two; it appeared to be a somewhat crude copy, perhaps made by a Celtic artisan to replace a lost or damaged Greek original.*

WHAT LIFE WAS LIKE IN IRON AGE EUROPE

In a forest clearing on the chalk downlands of southern Britain, half a dozen men and women emerged from the thatched round house that lay at the heart of their Iron Age village. They wore rough handmade shoes and garments woven from the wool of their own small sheep. Carrying long sickles, wooden forks, and stoutly woven baskets, they were bound for a sloping meadow where the sweet grasses stood ready to be cut. It was June, the season for hay making in the old Celtic farming calendar, and they tried not to notice the heat of the sun as they bent to their backbreaking labors. They also ignored the cameras and the sound equipment of the television film crew, assiduously recording their activities for a BBC documentary.

These particular Iron Age peasants were British men and women of AD 1977 who had answered a newspaper advertisement, placed by BBC producer John Percival, requesting human guinea pigs to take part in an extraordinary year-long experiment. They had been called upon to reenact, as accurately as possible, the daily life and work of a hypothetical band of Iron Age farmers, with their progress recorded in a series of television documentaries. Percival had long wondered how members of a highly urbanized, late-20th-century society would cope if thrust into the more rigorous living conditions of an earlier era. Would they be able to rediscover the

Tattered remains of two horsehides hang over a Danish bog at the Lejre Research Center. Archaeologists think that hides were ritually displayed in the Iron Age, as suggested by the presence at various ancient sites of horses' skulls, hooves, and leg bones.

practical wisdom and master the skills that had kept their ancient predecessors warm, well fed, and healthy?

"It was clearly impossible to recapture the beliefs and superstitions, the skills and experience, the basic social attitudes of prehistoric people," Percival has since explained, "but what we could do was re-create the living conditions, houses, clothes, food, and the hard, slogging labor that Iron Age people must have endured."

Percival's volunteers—six couples and two young children—would be left to their own devices in a remote corner of the countryside, on the grounds of a large private estate that allowed no public access. After a period of intensive study of existing knowledge about the arts, crafts, and technology of the Iron Age, they built themselves a homestead—a large circular communal dwelling with some outbuildings. Then they began to farm. Two days a week, a BBC film unit arrived to record the little community's activities over the course of four seasons.

When the year was over, the fire that had kept the homestead going was at last extinguished. Percival reflected that his band of villagers had made their own distinctive contribution to archaeological exploration, putting flesh on the dry bones of scientific data. "It is not enough," he said, "to know how a job may have been done. It is necessary to do the job day after day, to depend upon its being done satisfactorily to fulfill your everyday needs. It is necessary to live an experience in order fully to comprehend it."

Scholars have long exercised their imaginative and analytical skills on the thorny question of what life was like in the Iron Age. The literature of the classical Mediterranean world, in which the customs, worship, clothing, and even sex lives of the Celts are recorded, offers insights into their existence, but the works of course must be carefully evaluated for what they are—often prejudiced and distorted reports. Given the enormous number of Celts and their vast geographical spread, they left behind a great deal of evidence relating to their daily lives, including earthworks, potsherds, and the pieces of beautifully crafted metalwork that turn up from time to time in treasure hoards and graves. But much of what they produced for daily living has disappeared, largely because wood and wicker, two of the materials they commonly used, decay quickly and leave few traces.

Tangible remnants of the Celts' settlements may yet lie under the soil awaiting discovery, but the very terrain often retains the imprint of their plows, and the place names on the map carry memories of vanished tribes and lost sacred sites, encoded in their ancient tongue. Even their old gods and mysterious rituals survive by a slender thread in some areas, altered—but not totally severed—by newer systems of belief. In recent years a revolution in archaeological techniques has engendered an explosion of new or newly reinterpreted information about ordinary people, revealing that Celtic society was considerably more complex, more sophisticated, and infinitely more resourceful than was hitherto imagined.

Percival's modern Iron Age homestead is only one of a number of recent daily-life experiments; some have been on a far more ambitious scale. The vision for his project took shape during a visit to Denmark, when Percival found his way to archaeologist Hans-Ole Hansen's reconstructed Iron Age village at Lejre, in rolling farmland some 25 miles west of Copenhagen.

Hansen used archaeological and documentary data to get his project started in 1964. Every summer since 1970 a few Danish families have been invited to dress in the style of a long-vanished age, work with the utensils provided, eat the food, and cope as best as they can. In addition, experiments have been regularly carried out here over the years, some of them extremely practical. Just finding a way to keep the exterior clay walls of the houses from dissolving in rain and being eroded by the wind posed a big challenge. Farmers in northern Europe have long employed whitewash to prevent this from happening, but what did Iron Age peoples use? Years went by before a mix was finally achieved that worked as a protective coating. This consisted of gravel and cow dung kneaded together by hand, which was patted onto the walls and then covered with a clay wash that dried hard.

Another problem crying out for solution involved heating. As the people living in Lejre's wattle-and-daub houses found out, steady use of their fireplaces drew cold air into the room through cracks, lowering the overall temperature even as warmth rose from the fire, gathered in the cone of the thatched roof, and slid back down along the sides. Just by hanging a blanket between the living quarters and the attached stable they were able to raise the overall temperature by a surprising 68 degrees Fahrenheit.

A British counterpart to the settlement at Lejre was established in 1972 on Butser Hill in Hampshire, England, five years before the BBC's own experiment in Iron Age living got under way, and it continues to this day (pages 111-117). Called the Butser Ancient Farm Research Center by its founders, Peter Reynolds, a classicist turned archaeologist, and his colleague Jack Langley, it was designed as an open-air laboratory for research into the activities of Iron Age individuals. Both men supervised the erection of dwellings, barns, and other outbuildings according to plans deduced from past excavations. Encircling the structures with a ditch, bank, and palisade, they and their assistants planted fields employing Iron Age methods. When necessary, they used modern equivalents of prehistoric crops and supplied the site with those breeds of livestock most like the beasts that would have provided meat, milk, and wool to Iron Age farmers. The men had conceived of the project as a controlled experiment designed to last 20 years or more, which would allow them to test hypotheses and possibly solve some of the persistent archaeological puzzles about the Iron Age.

Reynolds and his team observed, for example, unexpected

ROUGH LIVING IN ROUGH TIMES

A teacher's chance discovery in 1933 of oak stakes jutting from a reedy portion of a Polish lake led to one of the greatest of Iron Age finds—remnants of a well-preserved walled town dating from around 550 BC.

Built on a five-acre island (now a peninsula), Biskupin was for 150 years a fortified settlement *(reconstruction, lower right)*. An outer palisade of 35,000 stakes driven into the muck at a 45-degree angle took the brunt of shifting ice floes in winter and thwarted enemy approaches. An inner wall, a log-and-earth rampart that reared 20 feet high and was topped by a palisade, had a watchtower

During the winter, families apparently brought their pigs and cattle into the vestibule in order to raise indoor temperatures. As perhaps another way of staying warm, they slept together, sometimes as many as 12 people in a bed.

A log-covered road ran from the town's gate and public square around the perimeter of the settlement. The parallel rows of houses were themselves separated by 12 corduroyed streets too narrow for oxcarts to pass *(below)*. In such close quarters, the threat of fire was always a concern, and the town appears to have burned on at least one occasion, perhaps set to the torch by marauding Scythians, fierce horsemen from the Russian steppes.

and piles of stone missiles positioned strategically along its 1,519-foot circumference.

The one thousand or so inhabitants—who tended lands close by—dwelled in more than 100 log houses. Each structure contained a single room with a loft for storing fuel and food and a vestibule. Entrances faced south to avoid the cold northwest winds and to receive maximum light and warmth from the sun, which the Biskupians probably worshiped as a god. Floors were covered with an insulating mat of alder and birch branches. Oval stone hearths—visible in the photographs at left and above—were used for additional heat and for cooking.

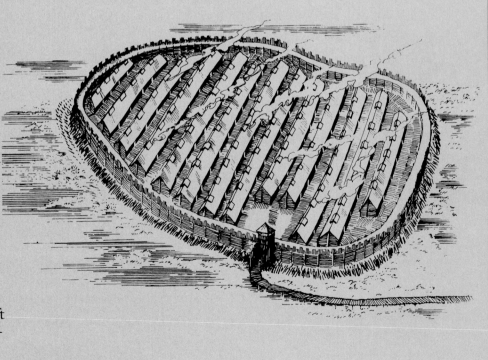

changes in a thatched circular hut, a replica of one structure excavated at the Celtic site of Maiden Castle, in Dorset. After the hut had been used to store grain and hay over a winter, hungry rats had tunneled their way in and created gulleys under the floor. Reynolds speculated that the so-called foundation trenches, which have been identified in many Iron Age buildings, may not in fact have been put there by the original builders but may have been added at some later date by rodent invaders.

While many discoveries at Butser occurred through such observations and in planned experiments, some were purely serendipitous. The scientists at the ancient farm, for example, may have stumbled upon the way in which Iron Age Celts learned how to make, from grain, the beer that has been attributed to them by classical authors. Following Iron Age custom, the experimenters had been storing their grain in pits dug in the chalky ground. Reynolds wrote of a winter with so much rainfall that "water penetrated into the pit and, of course, soaked the grain." Those who later scooped the wet kernels from the pit became somewhat tipsy from the fumes. It is possible, Reynolds speculated, that having found a certain pleasure simply in smelling such a weather-brewed concoction, Iron Age farmers might then have tasted it and decided to add some water to the mix to make it potable and a little honey to remove the bitter edge. "The effect of drinking it," Reynolds pointed out, "is just the same as drinking modern beer."

The growing interest in the field of experimental Iron Age archaeology has sparked a variety of research models. Some specialists have worked with ancient tools to re-create a particular manufacturing technique, such as metalworking. They have also duplicated the implements and agricultural practices of early farmers to assess their ability to feed themselves and safely store their surpluses for use in trade or to sustain themselves in the lean times between harvests. Each experiment has augmented knowledge of the period, although not always as anticipated.

Even the BBC's homestead offered unexpected insights for archaeologists. When Barry Cunliffe, a distinguished Oxford scholar of the Iron Age and the Celts, visited the settlement, he noticed little hollows of scooped out earth just inside the doorway to a house. These depressions, the residents informed him, had been made by the community's chickens, who liked to come in out of the rain on wet days and roll in the dry earth. "I can't now say," mused Cunliffe, "that every scoop I find in an Iron Age house is a dustbath for chickens, but it makes me understand, just that little bit more, the conditions under which people lived, and the range of explanations that are possible."

There are scholars, however, who have expressed doubts about the worth of such ventures. They argue that no matter how solid the scientific data upon which a reconstruction is based, it cannot be more than a work of the imagination. But the experimental archaeologists counter that the information garnered in such hands-on projects fleshes out the scanty data from excavations of settlements, where so much of the fabric of daily existence has been lost.

How, then, did the Celts live and cope, especially in a world of varying daylight, heavy rains, and often brutal cold? Diodorus Siculus went out of his way to comment on the weather: "In winter," he wrote, contrasting the northern climate with Rome's, "they have on cloudy days snow instead of rain, while in clear periods they have an extraordinary amount of ice and frost." Is it any wonder that he described their skin as pasty—"very moist and white"? Understandably, wool was a favored material. "They wear astonishing clothes," exclaimed Diodorus Siculus of the Celtic garments, "dyed tunics, displaying every color, and trousers that they call breeches. On top they pin striped garments made of shaggy material in winter, and smooth material in summer, divided into small squares of every shade." These cloaks were manufactured in Britain and Gaul until well into the Middle Ages. The first-century-AD Greek geographer Strabo notes that the garments commanded good prices and considerable respect when exported to the markets of Rome.

Archaeological remains do not contradict these reports. Excellent stitching and weaving are the most striking features of the few remnants of clothing that have survived from the period. Most of these examples come from burials in the preservative Danish bogs where scholars have found capes and tunics worn by men and the long skirts and sleeved blouses of the women. Trousers were uncovered in rich burial mounds of the late Iron Age.

A body that turned up in the 18th century in Yorkshire, England, wore a "toga of green colour, while some portions of the dress were of a scarlet hue, the stockings were of yellow and the sandals of a finely artistic shape." The clothing was in such good condition that

When this woman died in the third century BC, near present-day Zurich, she took her jewelry to the grave with her. Decked out in bronze, she wears rings on her wrists, ankles, fingers, and an upper arm, while 14 fibulae, or pins, lie on her chest. From rich graves such as this and using jewelry as a guide, scholars have noted trends in Celtic fashions. Between the fifth century and 250 BC, anklets increased from two to four, then disappeared; around 250 BC, bracelets of colorful glass replaced bronze ones. Other examples of Celtic jewelry are shown on this and the next page.

A late third-century-BC hollow-cast—and therefore lightweight—bronze armlet from the Tarn River in France probably encircled a woman's arm on special occasions.

Thought to be an import from Celts in the east, the piece expresses the abstract, vegetal style that would become a hallmark of Celtic art during the La Tène period.

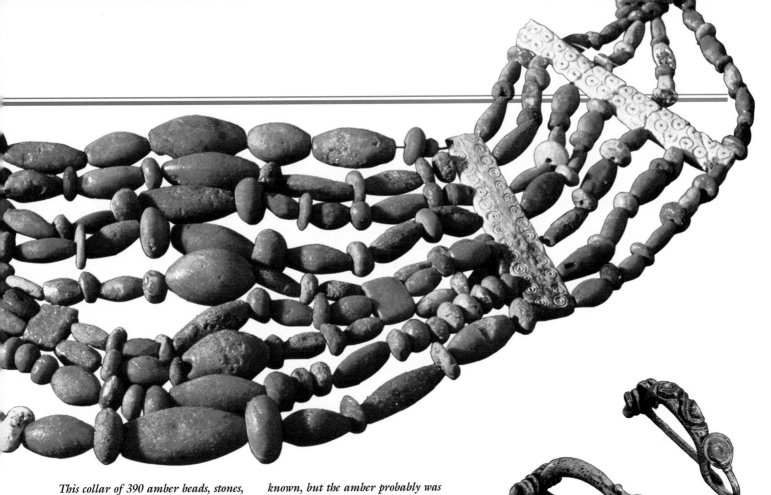

This collar of 390 amber beads, stones, and bone was discovered in a sixth- or fifth-century-BC grave in Austria. Whether the necklace was of local or foreign manufacture is unknown, but the amber probably was imported from what is now Poland. To satisfy the Celtic demand for the fossil resin, special north-south trade routes emerged.

Safety pins, or fibulae like these, were ornamental as well as practical. Some of the garment fasteners were designed with human, animal, or supernatural images; others were simply adorned with studs of Mediterranean coral riveted atop the catch plate, as seen above.

These glass bracelets owe their rich color to the inclusion of oxides. Cobalt yielded blue; copper, green; lead, yellow; and iron, red. Glass bracelets came into vogue in the last half of the third century BC. Blue ones, such as the example shown above, with its white and yellow decoration, were especially favored until about the first century BC.

some of the locals made off with items; it is thought that they sold the coat for reuse.

The looms that created this apparel have virtually disappeared, leaving their traces in a few combs for carding wool, some clay or stone loom weights, and most often, spindle whorls of baked clay. Some sites show postholes two to three feet apart in which uprights were set for the typical vertical loom. Such remains are often found in pits dug into the floors of houses. Placing looms in these holes enabled the weaver to increase the height of the loom, and thereby the length of the fabric.

One of the clearest pictorial representations of ancient European weaving is on a rudimentary rock carving at Val Camonica, near Milan, Italy. It shows a beam crossing the two uprights at the top of the loom, from which the threads hang, three rods crossing the loom to carry yarn for elaborate patterns, and a row of loom weights along the ground to hold the textile taut. Inventive weavers made good use of such equipment. And the Celtic love of color led dyers into the forests, rich in herbs and berries, in search of a wide range of plants; woad and madder, for instance, yielded blue and red, from which the weavers were able to reproduce an entire palette of purple shades.

To go with such finery, the upper classes sported an abundance of jewelry. Strabo describes Celts wearing "ornaments of gold, torques on their necks, and bracelets on their arms and wrists, while people of high rank wear dyed garments besprinkled with gold." From burials have come a dazzling assortment of armlets, necklaces, beads, brooches, as well as curiously wrought metal belts and rings for ankles and fingers.

Many Celts seem to have been fastidious about personal grooming. Archaeologists have uncovered the tweezers, razors, and hand mirrors that, according to classical writers, no self-respecting male or female could do without. Strabo suggests that an individual's looks could be the subject of considerable social pressure. Any young man who ran to fat and needed a girdle, or belt, in anything exceeding the standard size, was not just mocked and censured by the tribe but was forced to pay a fine for his obesity.

The great Greek sage Aristotle points out that Celts dressed their small children very lightly, despite the coldness of the climate. This practice, he explained, was a means of toughening the children, especially those destined to become warriors, who would need to shrug off physical privations in the course of battle. Artistic representations of these hardy Celtic fighters, created by their Greco-Roman opponents, offer a glimpse of the physical features, hair styles, and apparel that have been described in written sources.

The sites of thousands of Celtic settlements are scattered throughout Europe, but occasionally one commands attention for its outstanding physical features, such as Danebury, on the southern English chalk land of Wessex. Here, in 1969, British archaeologist Barry Cunliffe launched a long-term, intensive excavation of this English hill fort, an endeavor that would become a landmark in British Iron Age archaeology. Generations of farmers living within its protective walls occupied the spot for a virtually unbroken span of 450 years, from the sixth to the first centuries BC. The fort had three rings of defensive earthworks and enjoyed a commanding view of the downland, gently sloping fields of light soils that would have been receptive to their plows. As a further enhancement, it was located near a good source of spring water, an upland pasture for sheep grazing, meadows for cattle, a forest for sustaining herds of pigs, and easily accessible supplies of fuel and building materials, such as wood, straw, reeds, and clay, to keep the inhabitants warm and dry.

Cunliffe's dig was initiated at a turning point in archaeological understanding of the hill forts that dotted the English countryside and had fascinated scholars for centuries. Until the 1960s they were generally believed to be merely places of refuge for periods when indigenous tribes were

Excavation at the Celtic hill fort of Danebury, England, gets under way in 1969 with a cut through the main rampart and ditch (below). The kneeling figure works at the mid-sixth-century-BC ground level of the original wall, while the foreground figure stands in the ditch that fronted the wall. In a rebuilding phase centuries later, the ditch was deepened and cut in a V-shape, which gave the rampart a formidable 52-foot height.

pressed by other Celtic tribes. But by the time Cunliffe's first spade touched the soil of Danebury, archaeologists had shifted their focus from the massive walls of the hill forts to the people who had remained for centuries within their protective circle.

Cunliffe and his team first divided the entire hilltop into numbered and lettered squares and used this grid to record every posthole, pit, structural remnant, and artifact in its precise location. The digging began with a detailed investigation of the earthworks and the main gate into the settlement, in hopes of learning their construction methods, the order in which they were erected, and their probable dates and lifespans. The walls enclosed a 13-acre area of habitation, crammed with traces of buildings that included about 18,000 postholes. And its 5,000 storage pits contained a considerable amount of richly informative organic and manufactured debris.

Danebury seemed to have been laid out according to a systematic plan. This site, Cunliffe's team realized, was no random and primitive huddle of huts but a settlement marked by roads and paths as well as by orderly clusters of buildings, sited according to their use as homes, workshops, granaries, or shelters for livestock.

At a dominant position within the very center of the community, the archaeologists found evidence of one edifice markedly larger than the others. They were struck by the strong resemblance between this building and those found at settlements dating from the Roman occupation of Britain, which were widely believed to be religious shrines. One such temple, similar to that at Danebury, was uncovered during construction work at London's Heathrow Airport. The probable significance of the Danebury shrine was underscored by the fact that either this temple itself, or a sequence of similar structures erected consecutively on the same spot, remained in use throughout the nearly half-millennium of the hill fort's occupation.

But even the less important buildings incorporated good local materials and were apparently made to last. Houses were typical-

LAYING DOWN SUPPLIES FOR THE FUTURE

Thousands of large pits, like the ones seen at Danebury above, have been found all over Europe. While they seem to have been put to various uses, some yielded carbonized grain, suggesting they may have been employed for storage.

Experiments at Butser Ancient Farm Research Center in England demonstrated that the pits would have kept grain in good condition. Based on the average pit size—six feet deep and three feet in diameter—cylindrical test pits were dug into rock chalk ground, filled with about a ton of wheat each, and first covered with an airtight, raised, clay seal and then capped with earth to guard against runoff water (*diagram above, right*). Just before the storage pits were closed, sensors to measure temperature and gas

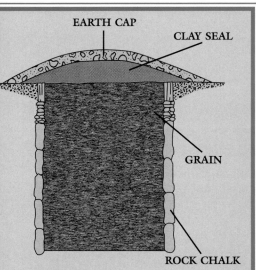

EARTH CAP
CLAY SEAL
GRAIN
ROCK CHALK

content were placed in the wheat (*below*).

The grain, left in the pits over winter, rapidly consumed the oxygen and released carbon dioxide. The increased carbon dioxide served to neutralize the microorganisms that would have caused the grain to rot. The Butser tests yielded less than two percent spoilage, all of it around the edges, a success equal to or better than that of modern storage systems. The remaining wheat was usable as food or as seed for the next planting. For the Celts, such results must have been tantamount to a life insurance policy.

ly circular, extending some 20 to 30 feet in diameter, roofed with thatch made of reeds, and walled either with vertical timber planks or wattle and daub. Doors, generally one to each house, were framed with sturdy oak. The inhabitants, mindful of the exigencies of the British climate, had taken care to weatherproof their homes, caulking gaps with moss and resin, using tongue-and-groove panels inside for a tight fit, and covering joints with extra planks to further prevent wind from whistling through. "There is no need to suppose that the structures were rustic hovels roughly lashed together," said Cunliffe, who instead suggests that the Celts' mastery of materials resulted in "stable structures finished to a high degree."

Excavations on the north side of the fort revealed traces of a structure identified as a house by its pair of domestic ovens as well as the carding combs and other small objects found within it. Because it was larger than the other houses, it might have been the residence of some individual or family group of higher social status; this deduction was reinforced by the discovery of a set of finely worked bronze harness fittings that had been lost or left behind when the house was finally abandoned.

Cunliffe and his team became expert in reading subtle clues. Detailed observation of the fort's vast number of postholes, for instance, suggested that while many were the remnants of supporting props for elevated oak granaries and similar large structures, others had been dug to hold a loom or a drying rack or to tether livestock.

Storage pits, found in the thousands all across the settlement, gave the archaeologists an increased respect for the practical wisdom of the Celtic farmers who had dug them. Most were bell-shaped craters, gouged as deep as 10 feet into the chalk of the hill; the marks of the iron adzes used to hack them out are still visible on the pits' inner walls. These pits were apparently employed to hold not only grain but also water, and they may have been used in brewing beer and in pottery production as well. As the excavation continued, it became obvious that they served a beneficial purpose; their sheer numbers gave the site the appearance of Swiss cheese. When, as inevitably happened, the ancient diggers of a crater found themselves cutting into an old silted-up chamber abandoned

by an earlier inhabitant, they reinforced its walls with flints set in clay or a neat arrangement of hand-cut chalk blocks.

Danebury's excavators could only guess at the probable population of the settlement, basing their assumptions on the total size of the enclosure and the estimated number of houses on the site. They reckoned that, at its peak, Danebury might have been home to some 200 to 350 people. That the community survived for so many generations testifies both to the site's natural advantages and to its inhabitants' intelligent exploitation of the environment.

Danebury was but one of scores of fortified settlements large enough to be classed as oppida in the entire European realm of La Tène Celts. In his annals of the Gallic Wars, Julius Caesar listed oppida belonging to 29 different Gallic tribes and regarded each oppidum as a political and commercial base of operations.

The largest of the oppida could sustain a permanent population of over a thousand and, in times of trouble, could accommodate many times that number in refugees from the hinterlands. According to Caesar, the oppidum of Avaricum, on the site of present-day Bourges, sheltered some 40,000 individuals during a Roman siege.

Almost inevitably, oppida were located upon commanding and easily defensible positions, such as a large hill or high plateau,

A restored remnant of the stone, wood, and earthen wall that encircled Finsterlohr, a second- to first-century-BC Celtic settlement on a south German plateau, shows its sturdy construction. The vertical posts, about 6.5 feet apart, are modern, filling the ancient postholes. The construction techniques used in building this type of barrier, known as the murus gallicus, *can be seen in the diagram at right of the wall at Manching, in Bavaria, a much larger Celtic settlement than Finsterlohr.*

with a sweeping view of the surrounding territory; a few were established at low-lying but equally strategic locations, such as the junction of two important rivers, thus offering a trade advantage as well. Their outer perimeters were well planned and strongly built, as at Danebury, and they were often made more formidable by wide ditches and tall banks that followed the contours of the site. It has been estimated that one individual, using an antler for digging and a willow basket for transporting the loosened soil, could have handled 35 to 46 cubic feet a day. Thus 200 people working side by side could have dug a ditch and thrown up a 13-foot-high tapered bank, 23 feet wide at the base, and topped it with a palisade of 1,000 stakes, in a relatively short 100 days. Plainly, such an effort would have taken considerable cooperation and organization, which has a great deal to say about the nature of Celtic society.

Walls varied. In Britain the mound type was favored, but on the Continent, ramparts tended to be reinforced with a wood framework and faced entirely or partly by wood or wattle, and sometimes by stone. The most famous kind, the *murus gallicus,* which even Julius Caesar found daunting, consisted of a backward-sloping earthen rampart, covered in front by interlocking stone blocks, reinforced with a wooden scaffolding packed with rocks and earth. The timbers were often fastened with iron nails 8 to 12 inches long; at one German oppidum, archaeologists figured that 300 tons of nails had gone into the wall's construction. The stonework made the murus gallicus relatively impervious to fire, while its rubble-packed timber framework resisted battering rams.

During times of peace, the walled oppida housed lively markets, multitudes of artisans, and even mints turning out coinage under the aegis of the local chieftain. In addition to the coins themselves, excavators have uncovered the ceramic molds used in manufacturing Celtic money. Alongside these visible relics of economic activity lay traces of the goods purchased with the money, such as iron

97

weapons; remarkably accurate devices for weighing and measuring; medical and surgical instruments; kitchen utensils; pottery produced on an industrial scale; tools for farmers and artisans in metal, wood, cloth, and leather; and even keys and locks for those affluent enough to have property worth stealing or who merely wished privacy.

In Germany's Bavaria, 20 years of excavations commenced in 1955 at the oppidum of Manching, under the direction of the German archaeologist Werner Kramer. Unlike many of its contemporary counterparts, Manching did not occupy an elevated site but was instead surrounded by bogs, which offered protection. The town stood alongside the Danube, a river that was an important European trade route, at the point where two well-traveled overland tracks crossed each other. When the walls were built, enclosing almost 939 acres of land (some of it apparently put to grazing use), their makers diverted the course of two streams to flow beside its outer ramparts, thus providing a further defensive element.

For about a century, between 150 and 50 BC, Manching flourished, probably housing between one thousand and two thousand people. Some of them were clearly engaged in the iron industry, as evidenced by large slag heaps—spoil from the smelting process that has been found in the boggy ground south of the settlement—along with many tools for forging iron, molds for casting bronze, and remnants of the blacksmiths' furnaces.

Armor and weapons, such as high-quality spears and swords, were a principal stock in trade for these Iron Age metalworkers. But the smiths also applied their skill to the creation of everyday items, such as wheel rims and iron hoops for wooden barrels. Alongside the busy smiths, other artisans were engaged in making glass beads and bracelets; both their finished products and the large chunks of glass that provided the raw materials have been salvaged by excavators.

At least some of the townspeople prospered sufficiently from such industries to import wine from the warm Roman south, as the inhabitants of Heuneburg had: More than 30 wine jars and amphorae brought to Manching from the Italian region of Campagnia have survived—although in shattered fragments—to attest to someone's fondness for the grape. The recipients

With potsherds abundant at many Iron Age sites, it seems natural that some of the kilns in which the originals were fired would crop up there as well. Examining such fragments, scientists can tell whether a pot was shaped by hand or on the wheel, how it was fired, and approximately how hot the fire was. Going further, they can analyze the composition of the clay and at times even pinpoint its place of origin.

Yet for all the information they may have collected about the pot, archaeologists still have to guess about the kind of kiln

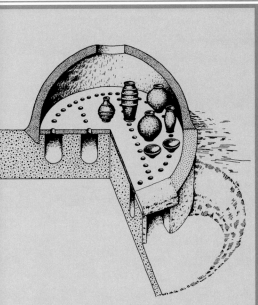

used to fire it. Few Iron Age kilns have survived, and the remains of the ones that have been uncovered are generally incomplete. Having been built outside of the settlements for fire safety reasons, they were destroyed over the centuries by agricultural activity.

To learn more about Iron Age kilns, archaeologists have resorted to trial and error and re-created several. At Lejre, in Denmark, a kiln *(left)* was dug into an embankment. High temperatures from the wood-filled firebox hardened pottery placed in the clay oven located over the heat source. By controlling the amount of oxygen reaching the fire, potters could regulate the temperature.

A more complex clay kiln of the late La Tène period is diagrammed above. Here, channels in the earth distributed the heat from the fire, which passed into the oven through a perforated stone plate. Depending on the amount of oxygen, the pottery could turn black, red, or red-black, the last a result of an oxygen-deprived atmosphere.

may have paid for these in locally minted gold and silver coins, weighed out on one of the 13 bronze-and-iron balance scales that archaeologists have brought to light.

Manching has yielded other evidence of its economic status. Archaeologists, finding prodigious quantities of animal bones, other food debris, broken pottery utensils, and many small-denomination coins that had apparently been dropped at random rather than hoarded, have hypothesized that Manching was a bustling regional marketplace, where traders congregated to do business while enjoying copious amounts of food and drink.

But the busy merchants and manufacturers of Manching were not to be allowed to go on wheeling and dealing in perpetual peace. For the excavations reveal that the oppidum came to a sudden and violent end. This sorry tale is told in the discarded iron weapons found scattered across the center of the town, as well as in the bones of hundreds of people, lying in chaotic heaps. Some of the skulls bore the marks of violent blows. The weapons themselves are of a style that scholars date from 130 to 50 BC, when Manching fell.

Although more and more people had come to live in oppida and to work there at various crafts, 95 percent of Europe's population during the late La Tène period is believed to have worked the fields—even some of the artisans themselves. From the archaeological evidence so far gathered, such yeomen seem to have been more than up to their agricultural tasks. Excavations at Danebury and elsewhere have indicated that Celtic agronomy was one of prehistoric Europe's great success stories. In their cultivation of cereal crops, Iron Age farmers of the late La Tène period achieved at least three times as high a yield per acre as did their medieval successors, working the same soils under similar climactic conditions. They grew three ancient types of wheat—einkorn, spelt, and emmer—which required far less nitrogen than their modern equivalents and, as botanists have determined, contained almost twice as much protein. Oat, rye, and millet were also planted, and buckwheat was successfully raised on high ground and poor soils inhospitable to wheat. Legumes too were an important resource: Lentils and peas could be dried to last out the winter, and the easily grown Celtic bean, high in nutritional value, may have been planted in alternate seasons on the same fields used for grains, as part of a system of crop rotation.

To prepare the earth, the early Celts used a light plowlike tool, called an *ard*, with a spiked end. Archaeologists have found the scratchlike marks of its passage over the ground in ancient fields, sometimes in a crisscross pattern that would seem to indicate the earth was plowed in two directions. Within the preservative peat bogs of the north, a few specimens of ards have survived. The most rudimentary were made entirely of wood, but in time they became more sophisticated; some versions were tipped with an iron shoe or fitted with iron plowshares that enabled the farmers to plow more land and to plow deeper, turning up the mineral-rich soil below.

Cattle provided the muscle power necessary to pull plows. Not only was a man's wealth measured in the number of these animals he owned, but the health and well being of the entire family were tied to them as well. Cow's milk was a principal source of nourishment, and pieces of broken pottery strainers uncovered at various sites hint at cheese production. Archaeologists have determined, after analyzing the animal bones found on Celtic sites, that beef accounted for more than half of the meat consumed.

But the Celts were also great lovers of pork and felt no feast or special celebration was complete without the chance to gorge themselves on the savory flesh of a fat pig. Salt pork from Europe's western fringes was sold as a great delicacy in the markets of Rome, suggesting that the well-known Irish mastery of the art of bacon curing may have a venerable pedigree. Wild foods too were served at the Celtic table. Medieval Irish storytellers knew they could make their listeners' mouths water by repeating the ancient promise made by the legendary hero Cuchulain: "If a flock of birds pass over the plain, you

Displayed above are materials and tools from an enameler's first-century-BC workshop at the Celtic settlement of Bibracte, now Mont Beuvray, in France. Among the items are crucibles, mortars, molds, tongs and spatula, ornaments awaiting decoration, and sticks and powder of colored enamel. At right is an example of Celtic enameling, a bronze harness mount. Though the mount is from a Gallo-Roman site in France, the design suggests it may have been British in origin.

shall have one wild goose and the half of another. If fish swim into the estuaries, you shall have a salmon with half of another. You shall have a handful of watercress and a handful of seaweed, and a handful of water-parsnip."

Cuchulain's bounty—including the seaweed, which was probably carrageen, a dark purple variety found on the shores of northern Europe—would have been cooked with some care, at least at the lavish feasts the Celts loved. The second-century-AD Greek writer Athenaeus told his readers that the Celts preferred their salmon baked, sometimes flavored with salt and vinegar or spiced exotically with cumin.

Like most Celtic activities, feasts involved elements of ritual, right down to the seating arrangements, which have been described by Athenaeus: "When a large number dine together they sit around in a circle with the most influential man in the center like the leader of a chorus. Beside him sits the host." On either side of these two the others were disposed in order of distinction. "Their shieldsmen stand behind them while their spearmen are seated in a circle on the opposite side, and feast in common like their lords." A note on the distribution of food is provided by Diodorus Siculus: "Beside them are hearths blazing with fire with cauldrons and spits containing large pieces of meat. Brave warriors they honor with the finest pieces." Athenaeus was struck by Celtic dining customs. "They partake of [the meat] in a cleanly but leonine fashion," he wrote, "raising up whole limbs in both hands and biting off the meat, while any part of which is hard to tear off they cut through with a small dagger which hangs attached to

Trays resting on makeshift stands hold sorted animal bones turned up in excavations at Manching, Bavaria, between 1955 and 1961. Almost all of the 400,000 fragments came from domesticated species—cattle, pigs, sheep, goats, dogs, and horses. Since only about two percent of the 938.6-acre site has been excavated, however, many more animal bones may lie buried there. Clearly, Manching's inhabitants—and visitors—enjoyed the meat of a variety of farm-raised animals.

their sword-sheath in its own scabbard." Diodorus Siculus humorously observed that "when they are eating, the moustache becomes entangled in the food, and when they are drinking, the drink passes, as it were, through a sort of strainer."

In 1979 Barry Cunliffe, at Danebury, uncovered a cache of ironwork that included two hooks forged with the skill of a master blacksmith, clearly designed to hang cauldrons over a fireplace, and also a set of iron spits for roasting joints of meat. "Who," wondered Cunliffe, "seeing the hoard and reading Diodorus's account of a feast, could really doubt the relevance of the classical accounts of Celtic society to the Iron Age of Wessex?" Not far from the place where these objects were found, Cunliffe had located the floor of a hut that had once housed the fireplace where such cooking would have been done; beyond the hut's vanished doorway lay refuse heaps filled with animal bones from countless meals.

Alcohol was important in Celtic festivities. Many classical writers comment, with undisguised contempt, upon both the amount of wine, mead, or beer consumed, and the revelers' tendency to move with alarming speed from friendly argument to inebriated brawl. But these gatherings were more than mere drinking bouts; there were tellers of tales, poets, and musicians to delight the company. An early Iron Age vase found at Sopron in Hungary, dating from the seventh or sixth century BC, is decorated with images of the lyres that such entertainers might have played.

At these festivities the Celts apparently behaved no differently than partygoers of most other eras: If they did not immediately fall asleep from the soothing notes of the harpers or the effects of too much drink, they might well find themselves in an amorous mood. But Diodorus Siculus saw fit to comment on some behavior he found strange: "Although their wives are beautiful, they pay very little attention to them, but rather have a strange passion for the embraces of males. Their custom is to sleep on the ground upon the skins of wild animals and to wallow among bedfellows on each side. The strangest thing of all is that without a thought of keeping up proper appearances they yield their virginity to others, and this they regard not as a disgrace, but rather think themselves slighted when someone refuses to accept their freely offered favors."

The beautiful Gallic wives may, themselves, have been busy at this stage of the evening, if a conversation overheard by Dio Cassius,

Astride his horse and armed with a spear, a hunter and his dog chase down a wild boar on a second- to first-century-BC miniature wagon, found at Mérida in Spain. At its chin, the horse wears a bell, perhaps to flush the prey from cover.

a Roman historian of the second century AD, is to be taken seriously. He tells of a Roman matron who accused a Celtic wife of promiscuity. The challenged Celt promptly countered with a feisty explanation of cultural differences regarding sexual practices: "We fulfill the demands of nature in a much better way than do you Roman women," she retorted, "for we consort openly with the best men, whereas you let yourselves be debauched in secret by the vilest."

Among the Celts' somewhat more down-to-earth pastimes was bird hunting; the old Irish tales report how the men struck the birds with stones from their slingshots or with a "wooden weapon" described by Strabo as "thrown by hand and not by means of a strap, with a range greater than that of an arrow."

Other favored diversions, for which there is archaeological as well as textual evidence, were board games and various outdoor contests between competing teams. A 1965 excavation of an Iron Age grave at Welwyn Garden City, just north of London, turned up a set of game pieces and dice, which archaeologists surmise may have been the components of an old Celtic board game known to chroniclers as *brandub*, or black raven. The upper classes, according to Irish lore, enjoyed a close relative of chess. They called it *fidchell*, or wooden wisdom, and it was played with two opposing armies of wooden pieces facing each other on a board.

Celtic outdoor contests, using sticks and balls, resembled modern hockey or games such as hurley and caman, still played in Ireland and the Scottish Highlands, in which teams of defenders try to prevent their opponents from getting the ball into a goal. A clay mold found on a Roman-British site in the English Midlands displays a naked figure carrying a ball and something that looks like a hockey

At right, a scene from a sixth-century-BC bronze situla, or wine bucket, found at Vace, in Slovenia, shows a musician playing the panpipes while a man holding a situla in one hand offers a cup of wine with the other. On the first-century-BC Kuffern situla below, from Austria, an embossed border celebrates athletic events, hunting, warring, and feasting. Though influenced by Etruscan designs, situlae are the products of northern workshops and provide glimpses into daily life in the Iron Age.

stick; the same equipment, also held by a nude sportsman, appears on a plaque from a diadem, which was discovered in the East Anglian village of Hockwold-cum-Wilton.

On a more practical level, what labors did the daily existence of the men and the women involve, and who performed them? An attempt to analyze gender roles was made by the British archaeologist David Clarke, who in 1972 reinterpreted the results of a dig carried out early in the 20th century at Glastonbury, in Somerset, England. He examined the earlier field reports and the artifacts collected from the excavated buildings for clues to whether the work done inside them had been tasks of men or women. Items found in large timber structures suggested male usage, for they included horse and chariot gear, weapons, a variety of workshop tools, needles, combs, and well-decorated pottery. Smaller houses held no traces of weapons or metalworking but contained enough evidence to indicate that spinning, weaving, grinding grain, and leatherworking had taken place there. These buildings he called "especial centers of female residence." His conclusions have been challenged, but many archaeologists believe there is a need to look for signs of women's roles in the workplace and investigate the division of labor in ancient Europe and elsewhere.

Intriguing images of women and men engaged in a variety of tasks and pastimes have been discovered on pottery at the Hungarian site, Sopron. The pieces may have been urns used to hold human ashes after cremation. Attempts at interpretation have been fraught with controversy. The figures assumed by some scholars to be female wear triangular flared skirts in vivid patterns, and their heads are adorned with what have been identified as either curly ringlets or large hooped earrings. Other individuals are clad in trousers.

The skirt wearers are engaged in spinning, weaving cloth, playing a lyre, riding on what appears to be an undersized horse, and dancing both singly and in a strange twosome that some have interpreted as a fight in progress. The trouser wearers herd or chase animals and lead a horse-drawn wagon. They too ride mounts of their own, but of bigger stature. Some archaeologists argue that the triangular garments might be cloaks rather than skirts.

Among the Celts there may well have been marked regional differences in the ways in which men and women related to each other. The tribes of Gaul, according to Caesar, made dowry arrangements that gave married women the same property rights as their husbands. "When a man marries, he contributes from his own property an amount calculated to match whatever he has received from his wife as dowry," the Roman wrote. "A joint account is kept of all this property, and the profits from it are set aside. Whichever of the two outlives the other gets both shares, together with the profits that have accumulated over the years." Gaul, however, was hardly a feminist utopia. In the same passage Caesar goes on to say that "husbands have power of life and death over their wives and children."

Whatever their status within the various societies of Iron Age Europe, women had full equality in the supernatural sphere. Celtic gods and goddesses constituted a sprawling, diverse band, and they were worshiped under many different local names and incarnations. Unlike the Olympian figures of the Greco-Roman pantheon, these divine beings did not belong to an orderly hierarchy with specific responsibilities and clearly delineated familial relationships.

The masculine deities, whatever their individual differences, seemed to be either avatars or descendants of a single, shadowy trib-

A GRUESOME FIND IN A SANCTUARY

The human bones at right—methodically stacked, some of them crisscrossed—present one of the great puzzles of Celtic archaeology. They were uncovered in 1982, along with a scattering of weapons, at the site of a Celtic sanctuary at Ribemont-sur-Ancre, France.

As the archaeologists examined the assemblage, they discovered that it consisted mostly of leg and arm bones that had been arranged in a square around what had been a post. Sixty percent were robust specimens, with grooves to show where heavy muscles had been attached. These bones had probably belonged to males. But the remaining 40 percent were thin and spindly, suggesting that they could have come from women. Some of the skeletal remains bore the nicks of weapons.

The archaeologists were confounded. Why had only long bones been piled up? What had happened to the rest of the skeletons, particularly the skulls? Could the bones have come from decapitated enemies, sacrificial victims, or dead Celts singled out for some sort of special treatment?

Diodorus Siculus, the Greek writer, claimed that Celtic warriors carried the de-

al father figure; the Irish tales identify him as the Dagda, "the Good God." Dagda was master of all the skills prized by the Celts, and their carved bronzes, decorated cauldrons, and sculptures show him in many incarnations—warrior, antler-crowned hunter, and bearer of a magic cauldron with the power to restore vitality and youth. Individual male gods are often illustrated as divine craftsmen, such as blacksmiths or, as in one stone carving from Germany, woodcutters. One of their number, Lug or Find, "the Fair-Haired One," is represented throughout Europe in place names and on dedicatory inscriptions.

The numerous goddesses worshiped by the Celts also emerge from a single being, a prototypical earth mother, the source of life and fertility but the mistress of chaos and its dark forces as well. This Great Queen had many incarnations and often appeared in the form of a trinity, expressing the Celtic reverence for the potent number three. From every corner of Celtic Europe have come visual and verbal representations of the Three Mothers. Sometimes, as in numerous reliefs found in Burgundy, they display such symbols of birth and fecundity as cornucopias or babes in arms; elsewhere, as in the dark world of the Irish legends, they are the terrible mothers of war, presiding over piles of bloodstained corpses on a battlefield.

Caesar found the Gauls "exceedingly given to religious superstition." In the forests, on the seashores, and upon the high moorlands of the Celtic landscape, otherworldly entities seemed never far away. Many birds and animals were sacred. Images of them crop up in Celtic art and oral traditions. There was the cormorant who drew the sun in its course, the swan who brought luck, the dangerous crane, the wild boar whose flesh sustained gods and heroes, the salmon who taught occult wisdom, and the mysterious serpent who wore the horns of a ram. At any time an animal of this bestiary could

capitated heads of their enemies home with them, preserved in cedar oil, and kept them in boxes to show off to friends; other ancient writers spoke of the victims' bodies being removed to sanctuaries and put on display, with the strict injunction that no one touch them.

Such questions so far have defied answering. But the inexplicable pile of bones is just one part of an area that has yet to be fully excavated, and it may yield other macabre relics and, archaeologists hope, information that will help to solve these mysteries.

serve as the fleshly host for some capricious, shape-shifting deity.

The landscape too was saturated with sacred importance. Rivers had their tutelary deities, and streams bore the names of their supernatural patrons. Scotland's River Clyde celebrates the goddess Clutha, whose sister divinity, Sequanna, bestowed her name on the great stream flowing through the heart of France, the river Seine. Sequanna presided over a healing spring at her river's source. Like many others throughout the Celtic world, the water's allegedly mystical powers drew pilgrims in the Roman era and well into modern times.

Excavations at Sequanna's spring, in a remote valley some 20 miles from the city of Dijon, have uncovered scores of votive offerings, produced from wood, bronze, and stone. Some represent humans, sculpted from the durable heart of the oak tree; others are images of different body parts and internal organs, including a plaque bearing an impressively accurate relief of the trachea and lungs. It quickly became apparent to the archaeologists that the objects were votive offerings, cast into the spring by pilgrims seeking relief from a variety of wounds or diseases. With the help of the goddess, or so apparently went Celtic belief, symptoms presumably would be transferred from the afflicted body part into its carved image.

At another French spring, near Clermont-Ferrand, the name of the governing goddess is unknown, but her sculpted personification as a seated matron survives. She probably was considered a specialist in treating eye ailments, for these organs figure largely in the collection of lovingly carved offerings deposited on the site by devotees. The devotees may have had good reason to pin their hopes on this particular fount, since an analysis of the water has revealed it to be rich in minerals known to have some therapeutic value.

To ensure that the rituals to placate their temperamental gods were performed properly and to interpret the mysteries of an environment steeped in magic, the Celts looked to the Druids. There were two major centers for Druidic education and training, one in the area of today's Chartres, west of Paris, and the other on the island of Anglesey off the coast of Wales. The Druids' duties, according to Caesar, were to "officiate at the worship of the gods, regulate public and private sacrifices, and give rulings on all religious questions." He noted that "young men flock to them for instruction and they are held in great honor by the people. They act as judges in practically all disputes whether between tribes or between individuals."

The historical truth about the Druids has been all but lost in a welter of myth and misinformation. But by sifting through the accounts of classical writers, it is possible to partially reconstruct their role in Celtic society. According to modern linguistic scholars, the name Druid may have derived from a word meaning either "profound knowledge" or "knowledge of the oak." Oak trees played an important part in Celtic religious practice. An oak grove was revered ground, one of the important sites for the conduct of religious rituals and ceremonies. The mistletoe, a semiparasite that grows upon the oak, was considered potent with magical and curative properties and was an essential ingredient in the performance of numerous rites, including the ritual slaughter of Lindow man *(pages 10-12)*.

Pliny the Elder, the first-century-AD Roman scholar, describes a Druidical ceremony for harvesting mistletoe. He recounts how two bulls, of purest white, are led to the oak where the precious plant grows. Then a white-clad Druid, armed with a golden sickle, climbs the tree and cuts the mistletoe, which he flings down onto a white

A seventh-century-BC bronze wagon, from a tomb in Strettweg, Austria, may depict a fertility rite. The central figure, a goddess, oversees the ritual before her as a duplicate scene unfolds behind. The stag is the intended sacrifice; its blood will be absorbed by the ground to ensure fertility and prosperity. The cauldron, borne aloft by the goddess, was restored in 1991.

robe, held up like a safety net by his fellow celebrants. As the bulls are sacrificially slaughtered, the group prays to the gods for whom the gift is meant. If these requirements are scrupulously observed—or so Celts believed—the mistletoe will have the power to render barren livestock fertile and to act as an antidote for every poison known.

Sacrifices of animals—and sometimes humans—had an important place in Celtic religious life. These killings were gifts to the gods as well as attempts to read the future. A scandalized Tacitus reports that the Celts' "religion enjoined them to drench their altars with the blood of prisoners, and to find out the will of the gods by consulting the entrails of human beings."

As teachers and scholars, the Druids in less bloody moments were also students of medicine, genealogy, and astronomy. Studying the cycles of the moon, they measured time by the passage and duration of the nights. The shape and rhythm of the year—punctuated, in part, by the great fire festivals of Samhain on November 1 and Beltane on May 1, when Lindow man may have gone to his death, as well as the lesser feasts of Imbolc and Lugnasad—were governed by a calendar that had been created by the Druids. As its sacred guardians, they dictated when crops should be planted or livestock brought to or taken from summer pastures, and they designated the dates most auspicious or ill-advised for waging war.

Almost miraculously, a relic of their knowledge of astronomy has survived. At the end of the 19th century, 100 broken fragments of an engraved bronze plate were found along a wooded riverbank at Coligny in eastern France *(pages 16-17)*. Scholars, reassembling the existing portions of the plate, were able to form a picture of its unbroken whole. The relic proved to be a calendar, originally five feet wide and three feet high, enclosed in a molded bronze frame.

The so-called Coligny calendar appears to date from around the second century AD and covers a five-year-long cycle of lunar months, each one divided into a dark and light portion, and each day numbered. Its makers used Roman numerals and Roman letters, but the words in the calendar—the names of the months and annual festivals and the designations of days as lucky or unlucky, "good" or "bad"—come from the ancient Celtic tongue. The calendar, at 2,021 lines, is the longest surviving Celtic text. From its shattered segments, the voices of the Celts themselves, free of the often biased interpolations of Roman chroniclers or Christian monks, speak directly to the modern world and tell us what they know.

FARMING THE PAST

Nestled amid the technologically advanced farms of southern England's highly productive agribusiness, within earshot of trucks and automobiles thundering along a busy main highway between London and Portsmouth, is a living echo of agriculture's vibrant Iron Age past. Here, no technique or tool invented during the last 2,300 years is ever knowingly employed.

This is Butser Ancient Farm Research Center, described by Peter J. Reynolds, its director for more than two decades, as an "open-air laboratory" where researchers re-create and study methods and structures thought to have been typical of Iron Age British farming. Thatched-roofed buildings and woven fences like those above are constructed as they were in about 300 BC—at least as far as can be discerned from available archaeological evidence, sometimes no more than faint patterns of postholes left in the ground. Crops known to have been cultivated by ancient

Britons (because of seeds accidentally burned to durable carbon millennia ago) are worked by muscle power—livestock or human. And while the Exmoor pony looking over the fence near the center of the picture is only believed to approximate the long-vanished short-legged Celtic horse, some of the farm's animals are of unchallenged Iron Age provenance. Soay sheep, for instance, were brought from Saint Kilda Island off Scotland, where isolation had kept their strain pure for two thousand years.

There are other reconstructions of Iron Age houses in Europe, but only Butser tries to re-create the actual agricultural processes that would have gone on in the fields around them. Although many thousands of visitors have toured the ancient farm, great care is exercised to protect the meticulously detailed experimental work from modern contamination. Even the neighboring farmers have agreed never to spray chemicals on their own fields when the wind blows toward Butser.

HARD WORK'S SURPRISING RESULTS

Finds of carbonized grains indicate that Iron Age Britons commonly grew two kinds of wheat: spelt and emmer. The Butser researchers set out to test this hypothesis and to gain insight into how much land and effort yielded how much grain.

The novice Iron Age farmers found the work hard. One of their problems, in fact, had never plagued ancient Britons—rabbits, which first came to England with the Norman Conquest. But from the start, the wheat results were what Peter Reynolds called dramatic. Even without the addition of manure as fertilizer, yields sometimes exceeded 1.1 tons per acre, sufficient to confirm the assertions of classical writers who said that Britain exported grain across the Channel to the Continent. Researchers acquired other new knowledge that only experiment could reveal. For instance, it was easier to pick the heads of grain from the standing stalks by hand than to harvest them with a sickle, previously thought to be the method used in the Iron Age.

Two Dexter cows (above) *cut the soil of a Butser field with a replicate ard. The farm chose Dexters because they are easy to manage and are similar in stature to the extinct Celtic shorthorn. Cows rather than steers are used for draft work because a cow, besides being strong enough to draw a plow, also* gives enough milk for a family, a fact that may have influenced ancient farmers as well. Unlike the moldboard of a true plow that turns earth over, an ard only stirs the soil. But some ards scored deep, as can be proven by the existence of these furrows in East Sussex dating from prehistoric times.

This wooden implement called an ard, some 2,400 years old, was found in a Danish bog. Iron Age farmers used such a tool to plow fields, often fitting the spike with an iron piece to reduce wear and increase efficiency.

Emmer wheat, a prehistoric strain with twice the protein value of modern bread wheat, flourishes in a Butser field. The straw from the wheat was used for thatching buildings like the round house pictured here.

Haystacks like the one above may explain a mystery: single postholes in the centers of shallow dishlike depressions at ancient farm sites. Butser haystack builders began with a vertical pole ringed by horizontal timbers (left) to lift the hay off the damp earth. A conical thatch cap protected the completed haystack from rain. The timber covering eventually killed plants below, causing the soil to subside slightly.

A HOUSE BUILT FROM PUZZLING CLUES

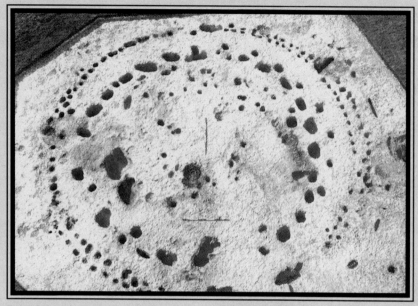

The Pimperne House excavation (left) *offered the builders few clues, its rings of postholes revealing little. It was the outermost ring of only six shallow, sloping holes that finally proved to be the key, when perceived as footing for six long, leaning rafters.*

The diameters of the posts below were calculated based on the corresponding holes at Pimperne, but their required heights at first were a mystery. It did seem likely that the ring of smaller poles could be the frame for a wattle-and-daub wall and that the larger posts might support rafters.

In 1976 the Butser center set forth on an awesome task: "the largest reconstruction of a pre-historic round house ever under-taken anywhere," said Reynolds. The job would be as much de-tective work and experiment as construction, since the only "plans" were some concentric rings of postholes uncovered at Pimperne, Dorset.

From these and other archae-ological clues, the builders man-aged to re-create a Celtic manor house some 42 feet in diameter. A two-person team did all the ac-tual construction. (Three would have been better, said Reynolds, and four, too many.) The project threw new light onto life in the Iron Age. It required 200 ma-ture trees, for instance, straight, 40-year-old oak and ash that in the Iron Age probably would have been taken from managed forests. This suggests not only a specialized timber industry but also a life stable enough for one generation to plan for the next.

The construction of roof framing (above) *was possible only after the dis-covery that six 36-foot-long rafters required butting into the earth for sta-bility. Prior to that, one of the heavy timbers toppled over, Reynolds said, "almost destroying half the work force"—that is, one of the two workers.*

A builder applies adobe-like daub to a wall of what became known as Maiden Castle House, named for the location of its prehistoric model. The mix, based on analysis of a fragment of daub uncovered at an Iron Age site at Maiden Castle in Dorset, includes clay, chalk, soil, straw, and animal hair. It is applied over wattle—branches woven around vertical poles.

This smaller structure at Butser, Maiden Castle House, is seen here with its roof unfinished to reveal the thatching process. Bundles of straw are lashed onto the roof in rings, starting at the eaves. Each ring of bundles overlaps the ring below to form a waterproof cover.

Hard by a beehive-shaped clay oven, a fire blazes at the center of Pimperne House. There is no smoke hole; the smoke filters out through the thatch, making storage for dried food possible by stifling oxygen up under the lofty roof. The farmer's indispensable ard is kept inside, behind the fire.

Puzzled by certain phenomena in the ruins of burned ancient houses—why, for example, had pottery fragments turned different colors—researchers hit on the idea of burning a re-created house to study the results. Denmark's Hans-Ole Hansen answered several questions by torching a meticulously crafted reconstruction in 1967. Hansen learned, for instance, that sherds can take color from a sod roof burning above, absorbing whitish ash from heather sod, or reddish ash from grass. In 1990 Reynolds set fire to a Butser house to study the effects. As can be seen here, they were quick, clear, and final.

Before the fire, the doomed building above appears sturdy. But only three minutes after a spark is purposely placed on its thickly thatched roof, as if it had leaped out from a hearth fire, *the structure belches dense smoke and flame* (below). *Soon billowing smoke fills the interior as well, creating a poisoned atmosphere that would asphyxiate a human being within 90 seconds.*

Only seven minutes into the blaze, temperatures of 1,000 degrees centigrade are recorded inside the already skeletal structure (above). *After 31 minutes* (below), *the frame, too, has* vanished in flames, and the conflagration ends. Rain soon brings down the daub walls, finishing the job of destruction. Later, one plowing of the site erases virtually all traces of the house.

HEROIC STRUGGLES
AGAINST
MIGHTY ROME

Carved in the Roman style, this legless limestone statue of a Celtic warrior in full battle gear—including chain mail, which may have been a Celtic invention— dates to the first century BC. It was found in southern France, a region that was heavily influenced by the Roman conquerors.

Although dwarfed by London some 20 miles to the southeast, the little city of St. Albans in the picturesque Hertfordshire countryside draws its share of tourists interested in antiquities. Among its attractions are remnants of a Roman wall that once surrounded the town, a fortification that bears mute witness to a grand if turbulent past: Two thousand years ago, when London was little more than a trading post, St. Albans—called Verulamium in those days—bordered the seat of Celtic high kings and was a valued outpost of the Roman Empire. It seemed apt, therefore, that archaeologists digging outside the northeast gate of the old town in the winter of 1991-1992 should come upon an astonishing find. So rich in remains and historical value was the discovery that Oxford archaeologist Martin Henig, an expert on Romano-British matters, described it as "the most important Celtic tomb ever found in Britain."

The tomb's occupant was probably a member of the royal family headed by Cunobelinus, according to Rosalind Niblett, keeper of field archaeology for St. Albans Museums and director of the dig. Important in his own day as the most powerful king in Britain, Cunobelinus was elevated to worldwide recognition when Shakespeare transformed him into the title character of *Cymbeline*. Moreover, his divisive family was as important to British history as it was to British literature. One of his sons, Caratacus, heroically led

Britain's Celtic resistance against invading Roman armies in the first century AD, while another son, Adminius, was placed on his father's throne by Rome as a lackey of the empire. Some archaeologists speculate that it was the bones of that very Adminius that lay in the St. Albans tomb.

Part of a five-acre, rectangular, ditched enclosure, the tomb stood on the crest of a hill. Pottery found at the site suggested a date of between AD 45 and 50—shortly after the Roman conquest of AD 43, and thus the right time frame for the burial of Adminius. The grave goods interred with the dead man bespoke the wealth and luxury that only Rome could have provided. Most of the objects had been damaged nearly beyond recognition from having been burned with the royal corpse on his pyre. Still, enough was left to indicate that he had lain on a couch adorned with ivory and silver, and that he had owned a 30-piece Roman dinner service, a silver-handled casket, a set of chain mail, and elaborate riding gear inlaid with enamel and bronze. Evidently he had also enjoyed Roman wine, for he took to his grave four Italian amphorae, each capable of holding more than two and a half gallons.

For all his Roman grandeur, however, the tomb's occupant did not lie in his final repose without reminders of his Celtic heritage. Diggers at the funeral site uncovered within its boundaries the remains of a Romano-Celtic temple, built some 40 years after the burial and clearly associated with the grave. It is believed that until the third century AD Celtic gods were probably worshiped there along with their Roman counterparts.

The grave told in microcosm the story of the waning of the Celts, of two cultures clashing, of the triumph of one and the death throes of the other. And if this was, indeed, the tomb of the collaborator Adminius, it was also a memorial to the Celtic factionalism that played so fatally into the hands of the Roman imperial strategy, *divide et impera*—divide and rule—the dictum that ended the long summer of Celtic preeminence in Europe. The tale was of powerful

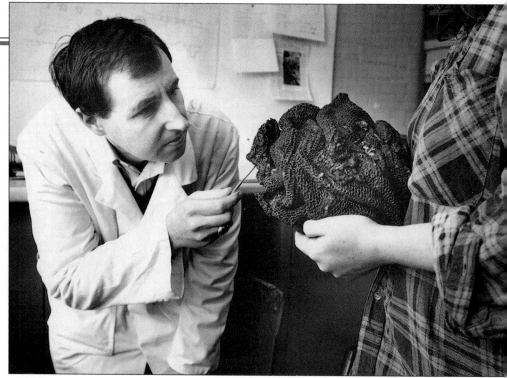

Philip Carter, a metals conservator at the Verulamium Museum in St. Albans, England, carefully probes the clump of chain mail discovered in the tomb thought to be that of the Celtic ruler Adminius, who died in the middle of the first century AD. The mail was fused together by the intense heat of the funeral pyre; its lumpy shape may be due to its having been tied up in a bag at the time of burial.

personalities both Roman and Celtic, desperate armies, and terrible retribution, as one side fought for glory and empire, the other for the survival of their ancient ways. Ironically, it is in this period of Celtic decline that the Celts come into sharpest focus, their exploits and defeats having been chronicled in detail by the ancient historians.

The beginning of the end occurred not in Britain but across the English Channel in Gaul. Through trade and war Celts had made their presence felt from Asia Minor to the British Isles, but by the start of the second century BC the expansion was waning. The Celts had settled into the lands they had previously raided, built urban centers, and now often were the invaded rather than the invaders. Celts in what are now Austria, southern Germany, and western Hungary were beginning to feel the pressure of Rome and would later be assimilated into Rome's burgeoning empire. Fertile Gaul in the west, the Celtic heartland, was being squeezed not only by Rome, to the south, but also by forces from across the Rhine River, where the threat came from land-hungry tribes that Greek and Roman historians called Germans *(pages 122-123)*.

It was a German named Ariovistus, king of the Suebi, who in 71 BC figured in a lethal trinity of troubles for the Gallic Celts. With tribes to his north craving more territory, Ariovistus was looking for new land for his people when fate seemed to offer him a windfall. On the Suebi side of the Rhine, the Gallic Sequani tribe called on Ariovistus to intervene in its long-standing squabble with the rival Aedui, also a Gallic tribe. Ariovistus was more than willing, provided that the Sequani would grant his people land in what is now Alsace. The pact was made, and by 61 BC Ariovistus had defeated the Aedui and had started wholesale raiding into Celtic territory. At this point, the Aedui chieftain Divitiacus appealed for help to Rome.

The plea for aid from the south was not surprising, since Rome, through a combination of conquest, colonization, trade, and diplomacy, had become a force in southern Celtic lands. Territory in northern Italy, once dominated by Celts, had long since fallen to Rome and had been officially annexed in 82 BC as the Roman province of Cisalpine Gaul. West of the Alps, Rome had established what it for a time called simply the Province—which lent its name to modern Provence—extending over Celtic territory between the Alps and Massilia, and north almost to Lake Geneva. By 118 BC the area

121

had been pushed westward to the Pyrenees and Toulouse, and the Province was renamed Gallia Narbonensis. Within its confines the Celts increasingly adopted Roman dress and manners. To secure its stronghold further, Rome sought alliances with a number of tribes along the northern border of Gallia Narbonensis, notably Divitiacus's powerful Aedui.

This Gallic tribe might well have gotten the help it needed against Ariovistus, but the year was 59 BC, and the second element in the conflux of factors that would augur doom for an independent Gaul arrived in the person of Gaius Julius Caesar, consul of Rome. A year later Caesar was named governor of Cisalpine Gaul and Gallia Narbonensis. A patrician by birth and temperament, he was a military genius as well as pragmatic, ruthless, and enormously ambitious. He saw the suppression of Gaul as the pathway to further glory.

Glory, however, lay in the telling as well as the doing, and Caesar was not going to leave his story to the able if sometimes acid pens of Rome's historians. He decided to preempt their moves as neatly as he would those of an opposing army. To this end he would write seven accounts of his upcoming campaigns, to be called *Commentaries on the Gallic Wars.* They would be published in Rome, a volume each year between 58 and 51 BC, thereby providing not only a paean to his own prowess but also the most detailed report known of ancient warfare. Obviously biased, Caesar's account belittles Celtic victories and stresses the alleged deceitfulness of the Gauls. Nonetheless his war stories have held in thrall generations of readers and have proved a reliable guide for excavators digging at various battle sites.

Despite his desire for the acclaim of his fellow Romans, Caesar considered it more advantageous, for reasons meshed in the snarl of Roman internal politics, to persuade the Senate to ignore the Aedui plea for help against the Germans and to side instead with Ariovistus. The German chieftain was thus declared "king and friend of the Roman people" and was left alone to pursue his predations against the Gauls.

While all this was going on, the large Celtic tribe of Helvetii in what is now Switzerland was preparing for a mass migration. Pressed, like others, by Germanic incursions from the north, and mindful of voracious Rome to the south, the Helvetii wanted to move west to get away from Germans and Romans alike. So, according to Roman accounts at least, early in 58 BC almost 400,000 people—the Helvetii and several other tribes—set off for

JUST WHO WERE THE GERMANS?

Characteristically Celtic in design and feeling, the glowering face at right was one of four adorning a first-century-BC wagon found in a Danish bog. Since Iron Age Denmark was a Germanic land, the Celtic style of this work poses a question: Were the Germans Celts, or, at the very least, were the early Germans as referred to by ancient Greek and Roman writers the direct ancestors of today's Germans? Probably not. Most likely they were a mix of German, Celtic, and other groups. Up until the first century BC northern Europeans were commonly considered either Celtic or Scythian by the Greeks and Romans. Indeed, the Germans were not even recognized as a distinct group.

Julius Caesar, in his war commentaries, is the first writer to give a detailed description of the Germans that clearly distinguishes them from the Celts. In contrast to the "semicivilized" Celts, Caesar depicts the Germans as more primitive and rugged: "All their life is spent in hunting and in the practice of the art of war," he writes, "from childhood their aim is toil and hardship." Caesar even goes so far as to set the Rhine as a line of demarcation between the two peoples, Germans to

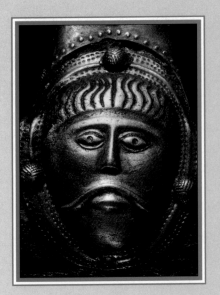

the east and Celts to the west.

However, Caesar's motives for making such a sharp distinction between Celts and Germans are suspect. His own writings show that Celt and German tribes often intermixed with little regard for ethnic and geographic boundaries. And just as the Greeks, Etruscans, and Romans heavily influenced the Celts of the Iron Age, so did the Celts influence the Germans. German leaders often had Celtic names. Even the names associated with Germans appear Celtic: Teutones was the Celtic term for people in general, while Germani is believed by some scholars to have been a Celtic tribal name.

Nevertheless, from Caesar's time onward, German becomes the name commonly given to all people dwelling east of the Rhine River, especially to marauders of any ethnic stripe who were crossing the Rhine into Roman Gaul.

new living space in western Gaul, after setting fire to their homes.

The Helvetii had received permission from the Sequani to move through their territory on the westward march. But the Aedui complained of Helvetian pillaging in their land, and their chieftain Divitiacus once again appealed to Rome. This time Caesar, delighted with the opportunity for direct intervention in Gaul, decided that the Aedui were Rome's allies after all. He set out after the Helvetii with six legions, finally ambushing them at the Aedui capital of Bibracte, on Mont Beauvray near the modern town of Autun in eastern France. In two days of fighting, three-fourths of the Celtic émigrés—men, women, and children—were slaughtered. The surviving Helvetii were forced to return to the charred remains of their homes.

Caesar's brutal thoroughness made a powerful impression on a number of the Gallic chieftains, and they hastened to ask him again to help rid them of that erstwhile "friend of the Roman people," Ariovistus. Caesar had no trouble gaining Rome's approval for the venture and, without a qualm, Ariovistus's one-time backer ordered the Suebi chieftain back across the Rhine, since all of Gaul was now under Roman protection. Predictably, Ariovistus declined. Battle was joined in Sequani territory 100 miles northeast of Bibracte, where the Germans were routed. The immediate threat to Gaul was thus averted, but at exorbitant cost. At the Celts' own invitation, the more dangerous enemy, Rome, was now firmly entrenched among them.

From 58 to 53 BC Caesar cut through Gaul like a scythe through a wheat field. His advantages lay in his strategic prowess and his efficient, disciplined legions. The Celts fought with consummate bravery, but they were handicapped by their martial traditions that relied more on individual valor than on strategy and tactics. They were also hobbled by their tribalism. Against a unified foe, the provincial, independent Celts could not—until it was too late—make common cause against the enemy.

In 57 BC Caesar turned his attention north toward the Belgae, a confederation of tribes that he regarded as the toughest of the Celts and therefore a threat to Roman interests. A bellicose and spartan people, the Belgae were, as Caesar noted, "farthest away from the culture and civilized ways of the Roman province." Intensely independent and anti-Roman, the Belgic tribes armed themselves. Nevertheless, in a single season Caesar crushed them, although the Belgae would always remain restless and prone to revolt. The fiercest of the tribes, the Nervii, he virtually annihilated, leaving only 500 survivors from a force of 60,000.

Caesar, in only two campaigns, had succeeded in bringing much of Gaul to heel. The only major area left to deal with was Armorica, on the Breton peninsula, and Rome's master general effectively quashed dissent there by defeating the maritime Veneti tribe and their allies in a naval battle in 56 BC. His pretext for attacking the Veneti was that the tribe had detained two Roman envoys. In retaliation after defeating them, Caesar had all the tribal leaders killed and the surviving warriors sold into slavery.

So secure did Caesar feel in his triumphs that in 55 and 54 BC he ventured to make expeditions into Britain. The two forays were not especially important militarily—Britain would have nearly a century's grace before feeling the full force of Roman might—but they did play well back home, as Caesar undoubtedly knew they would. But in September of 54 he returned to Gaul to find the land in turmoil, seething with rebellion.

The leader of the Celtic revolt was Ambiorix, king of the Eburones, a Belgic tribe whose land lay between the Meuse and the Rhine Rivers. Ambiorix had rallied the smarting Belgae to his cause, along with several tribes south of the Seine and some discontented Germans from across the Rhine. In Caesar's absence, Ambiorix and his troops managed to beat a Roman legion. But when Caesar attacked the rebels in the summer of 53 BC, the result was ruinous for the Celts. Ambiorix escaped, though his army was decimated. The Romans razed every enemy village, confiscating crops, slaughtering livestock, and leaving the rebellion's survivors to starve to death. But even this disaster did not quell the spirit of revolt in Gaul. On the

On this narrow neck of land jutting into the Atlantic off Brittany, the Veneti tribe built one of their many fortified settlements, protected against assault by high cliffs, rough seas, and a line of trenches athwart the mainland approaches. In 56 BC Julius Caesar at last defeated the Veneti by luring them into a sea battle in which their sturdy, sail-driven boats proved useless when the Romans, manning oared war galleys, cut the riggings.

contrary, it seemed to inflame it, for only one year later the Celts would be inspired by a leader who would give them their last, best chance to escape Roman domination.

His name was Vercingetorix, a young aristocrat of the Arverni tribe whose capital was the oppidum of Gergovia on the Allier River near modern Clermont. Although excavation shows Gergovia to have been urbanized for only a few decades in Vercingetorix's day, its inhabitants nonetheless appear to have been well off, their feasts enhanced by Greco-Italian wines and the widely disseminated black tableware from Campania in Italy. So it must have been a blow to Vercingetorix when he was expelled for his anti-Roman sentiments. He soon gathered a band of followers, however, and returned to Gergovia, where he ousted the opposition and installed himself as king.

In Vercingetorix the Celts had a compelling personality as well as a leader whose gift for strategy seemed almost a match for Caesar's. He was recognized by Caesar as "a man of enormous energy, but also a very strict disciplinarian." The new chieftain made his advent at a propitious time. By now almost all of Gaul was so outraged by Caesar's punitive methods that the Celtic leaders came as close as they ever would to forming a unified front. Even the Aedui, Rome's closest Gallic allies and its original gateway into Gaul, were now staunchly anti-Roman. In the autumn of 53 BC, after Caesar left for Italy as he normally did following each summer campaign season, an assembly of Gallic tribes accepted Vercingetorix as its leader and began laying plans. Vercingetorix's strategy was to prevent Caesar from reentering Gaul and thus cut off the main Roman force, wintering in Belgic lands in the north, from its leader. The Celtic rebellion broke out in the winter. As soon as Caesar heard about it he hastened back across the Alps with fresh troops from Italy, picking up reinforcements in Gallia Narbonensis. Marching day and night, he hurried along the Rhone and Saône valleys. The campaign that was to follow has been called by some scholars the war of the oppida, for its major battles took place at a series of these urban centers, which were attacked, occupied, or demolished.

In preparation for warfare, Vercingetorix ordered a scorched-earth policy to deprive the Romans of food and supplies. The Biturges tribe resisted, refusing to burn their capital, Avaricum, which they held to be, according to Caesar, "the most beautiful town in Gaul." This oppidum was identified in the 19th century within the modern city of

READING THE TELLTALE SIGNS OF AN IRON AGE MASTERPIECE

In May 1891, peat cutters near the Danish village of Gundestrup uncovered the dismantled pieces of a silver cauldron embellished with more than 100 figures of animals, gods, and soldiers on foot and on horseback *(below)*.

The first examinations revealed that the vessel was 97 percent pure silver, weighed almost 20 pounds, and measured 27 inches wide. More recent microscopic investigation has shown that it was once gilded to highlight details. But its place of manufacture has long eluded investigators. Guesses range from Gaul to Russia; Thrace, in the Balkans, now seems the likeliest spot. There a Celtic tribe known as the Scordisci settled; examples of Thracian silverwork bear stylistic and technical similarities to the cauldron. How the vessel came north remains a mystery, though it could have been seized as booty by marauding Danes.

Through careful analysis of punch marks left by the silversmiths who embossed the vessel, a Danish scholar has identified the "signatures"—microscopic irregularities indicating distinctive tools and hammering methods—of five different artisans *(bottom right)*. He hopes one day to match them to those on other pieces and settle the provenance debate once and for all.

These precise facsimiles of the Gunde-strup cauldron's panels were made in 1977, when the vessel was taken apart for conservation. Scholars still argue about how the plates should be arranged, a task made more difficult by the fact that one of the eight exterior panels is missing.

Some scholars maintain that this silver plate, dominated by a bull, was origi-nally a decorative plaque on a horse harness. It may then have been used to plug a hole in the cauldron's bottom.

Microscopic analysis of punch marks shows the distinctive hand of one of the five silversmiths who decorated the vessel. At far left, for example, is a detail of the half-circle marks used to represent the hair of the bull in the plate shown above; as seen at near left, each mark bears along its middle the same peculiar clump of minuscule round irregulari-ties unique to the smith. Scholars now date the cauldron to around the first century BC, which makes it possible to compare its style and technique with that of other metalworks of the same period.

This full-scale reproduction of a section of the siegeworks thrown up by Julius Caesar's legions during their attack on Vercingetorix's hilltop stronghold at Alesia was built as part of an open-air cultural theme park in Beaune, France. The towers rear 29½ feet high. The sharpened stakes bristling out of the ground in front of the fortification were only one of several kinds of impediments designed to slow the advance of enemy forces.

Bourges, the center of a region that had particularly rich soil and an abundance of iron ore, which was probably a major source of the community's wealth.

Suddenly, before Vercingetorix could intercept him, Caesar crossed the Loire, and his troops surrounded Avaricum and laid siege to it. In less than a month his soldiers built two 80-foot-high wheeled siege towers and the 400-foot ramps over which these would roll. They also constructed a roofed terrace, 80 feet high, for such artillery as catapults and mounted crossbows that could shoot iron-tipped arrows; in addition, hundreds of javelins would be thrown from this perch onto the trapped defenders.

In his writings, Caesar pays tribute to the "ingenious" Gauls who, while the Romans were building their ramps and siege towers, "were making constant sorties, day and night, and either setting fire to our terrace or attacking our soldiers when they were at work there." He also commends the near-legendary heroism of the Gallic defenders by recounting an incident he considered "so remarkable I must not leave it out." It happened one night during a battle that raged after the Celts had tunneled under the Roman siege terrace and set it afire: "One Gaul stood in front of the gate of the oppidum taking lumps of tallow and pitch that were handed to him and throwing them into the fire opposite one of our towers. He was pierced in the right side by an arrow from a catapult, and fell dead. Another Gaul, standing nearby, stepped across the body and did the same job." When he too was killed, a third and then a fourth man took his place, and so on into the night. "The post was not abandoned by its defenders until the fire on the terrace had been put out, the enemy pushed back at every point, and the fighting brought to an end."

Eventually Caesar overran the oppidum, killing all but 800 of its 40,000 people and selling the survivors as slaves. This disaster convinced wavering Celts of the wisdom of Vercingetorix's policy to deny the enemy the provisions of the towns, and the Gallic nights began to glow with the flames of farms, villages, and some 20 oppida torched before the Roman advance.

Caesar, now reinforced with six legions, decided to strike at Gergovia itself. The settlement stood on a high plateau between two rivers, and on this advantageous terrain Vercingetorix made a stand. Positioning his army outside the walls to prevent a siege like the one at Avaricum, the Celtic leader managed to fight off a Roman assault. Then he counterattacked, pressing his own offensive with such success that the Romans were routed, losing 46 of their officers and 700 men. Word of the victory traveled through the country: A Celtic leader had bested the great Caesar. At this, even the few submissive tribes who had promised Caesar provisions began destroying the supplies earmarked for Roman troops.

But Gergovia was the apogee of Celtic resistance. Shortly thereafter, Caesar was able to reunite his two armies and turn them toward the destruction of the rebels. After German mercenaries defeated the Celtic cavalry, the Romans cornered Vercingetorix's forces at the hilltop fortress of Alesia, near what is now Dijon.

Alesia stood on a large diamond-shaped plateau with steep hills on the north and south and open country to the west. It was, like Gergovia, protected by streams on two sides. Archaeologists believe Alesia may have been the center of a cult of Epona, a goddess on horseback—a statue of this deity riding sidesaddle was found at the site—and the Celtic warriors assembled there may well have besought her for aid. If so it was in vain, for now Vercingetorix, with only 50,000 men, was penned inside the walls and outnumbered more than two to one. Moreover, Caesar had learned his lesson at Gergovia. Rather than storm Alesia, he threw up siegeworks.

Vercingetorix called his chieftains together to discuss options, and it was clear that the spirit to resist was not wavering. According

Struck at a Celtic mint in 52 BC, the gold coin at top displays an idealized portrait of the chieftain Vercingetorix, who was then in the throes of his bold revolt against the Roman invaders of Gaul. In 48 BC, just three years after his defeat, a Roman silver denarius (above) showed what some scholars believe is the less flattering image of Vercingetorix as a wild-haired, fiercely bearded Celt.

to Caesar, one Arvernian noble even suggested at this conclave that the army resort to cannibalism, eating those too young or too old to fight, rather than surrender.

The Celts harried construction of the Roman siegeworks as best they could, trying to buy time while Vercingetorix sent forth a call for reinforcements. The call met with an overwhelming response: Some 240,000 Celtic infantry and 8,000 men on horseback gathered on the plain west of Alesia to try to raise the siege. But after three days of savage fighting, the Celts were soundly beaten and the remnants of their army scattered. Vercingetorix and his men, who had tried to break out of their fortress, were forced back inside the walls to face almost certain starvation.

Vercingetorix then called a council to discuss the grim prospects faced by both the warriors and Alesia's civilian noncombatants, whom the Romans had not allowed to leave the town. He put his fate in the hands of the tribal leaders, saying he was willing to be handed over to the Romans, dead or alive, to stave off what was otherwise sure to be bloody retribution. In the end, it was decided to send a deputation to Caesar to discuss terms of surrender. The discussion was short; the terms were unconditional submission.

Vercingetorix was hauled off in chains first to Bibracte, where Caesar remained with his army for the winter, then to Rome to languish five years in prison. In 46 BC the Celtic leader was publicly beheaded as part of a celebration of Caesar's triumphs. In 40 BC a likeness of that head was struck on a Roman silver coin to commemorate the defeat of Gaul.

More than 1,900 years later, in 1860, another military man, Colonel E. Stoffel, his mind crammed with Caesar's details of the siege of Alesia, searched for the site and found it on Mont Auxois, near today's Alise-Ste.-Reine. He had been sent by Napoleon III, who in that same year had initiated a series of excavations at French sites thought to be forts and battlefields in the Gallic Wars.

With the assistance of 300 workers, Stoffel burrowed into the terrain surrounding Alesia's high plateau, where he found traces of Caesar's siegeworks, such as postholes and other imprints in the soil. Based partly on Stoffel's work, an imaginative reconstruction was later built in 1978 at the Archeodrome, a kind of historical theme park at Beaune between Paris and Lyons *(page 128)*. A hoard of coins unearthed at Alesia includ-

REAL-LIFE ECHOES OF EXCALIBUR

It is one of the most dramatic moments of medieval legend. Mortally wounded in battle, the great sovereign King Arthur commands a loyal knight to take the enchanted sword Excalibur and hurl it into a nearby pool. When the knight obeys, the hand of the mysterious Lady of the Lake appears and pulls the mighty weapon beneath the waters *(right)*. There Excalibur awaits the grip of a risen Arthur, come at some future time to drive his people's enemies from the realms of Camelot.

This stirring tale contains a grain of truth: Just as there must have been a sixth-century-AD British-Celtic ruler, or rulers, who inspired the enduring Arthurian legends, hundreds of Celtic swords have been recovered from pools, lakes, and bogs.

The bronze swords shown below were among some 80 to

90 blades retrieved in 1975 from a marshland at Gournay-sur-Aronde in northern France, an area bordering the former domains of three powerful Celtic tribes. Most of the blades were notched, broken, or, like the ones seen here, bent. Scholars believe this may have been done deliberately, as a kind of

ritual killing of the swords upon the deaths of their warrior owners. The now useless blades were then sacrificed to the waters, where they lay undisturbed until modern times.

The romance of Arthurian legend has long captured the imaginations of archaeologists. One English site that has received their attention is Cadbury Castle, an 18-acre hill fort. Could this have been Camelot? Excavations have uncovered evidence to link it to Arthurian times, but suggest that it may have housed an army rather than a band of merry men.

ed some minted by Vercingetorix, bearing his name. This site of the final Gallic defeat became, after the conquest, a major Roman town. As further digging would reveal, its streets were laid out in a typical Roman grid, with temples, a theater, a forum, and a basilica, all erected in the grand style of the conquerors.

Further evidence of Roman military engineering at Alesia and elsewhere has been obtained through aerial photography. The lines of Caesar's siegeworks have shown up clearly in infrared images, and several Roman camps have been discovered by using this method.

Other oppida that figured heavily in the Gallic Wars, such as Bibracte, Avaricum, and Gergovia, were also located in the 1860s. In 1867 the French archaeologist J. G. Bulliot began digging at Bibracte. The excavation was continued by Bulliot's nephew, Joseph Dechelette, at the turn of the century. Dechelette uncovered the remains of a town with streets and housing areas divided into specialized quarters that included a region for religious activities, a district of workshops and artisans' houses where metal was forged and enamel was made, and a residential area of more-substantial houses for the upper class. The town center boasted a market and spaces reserved for meetings and ceremonies.

After his Gallic victories, Caesar would go on to new adventures. He spent two more years in Gaul, mostly in punitive and mopping-up expeditions. Dissent was not entirely broken; there were uprisings here and there to be put down. But for all practical purposes, free Gaul died at Alesia. Then Caesar went home to win a civil war and achieve his grand ambition of becoming Rome's dictator for life—a short life, as it turned out, since he died by assassins' daggers in 44 BC. His legacy in Europe was an increasingly Romanized Gaul, but even as many Celts were losing their ancient identity, there were others in more remote areas who proudly clung to it.

Sir Mortimer Wheeler, modern Britain's archaeologist extraordinaire, was not unlike Caesar, whose ancient footsteps he dogged. Both Wheeler and Caesar were brilliant scholars, and both were splendid soldiers, Wheeler distinguishing himself in the two world wars. Each had formidable presence and a passion for command, and each was colorful and knew the value of public relations.

Caesar's account of his expeditions into Britain helped prompt Wheeler in 1929 to begin four years of excavations in and around the old Roman town of Verulamium. The archaeologist had high hopes of finding traces of pre-Roman habitation by members of the Belgae, only one of several Celtic tribes that had branches in Britain. Many of the Belgae had migrated to Britain by the first century BC. They brought with them a La Tène culture more advanced than that of the native British farmers, along with trade ties to the Continent. Belgic burial sites, such as one found at Colchester in 1924 and the recent find at Verulamium, have provided evidence both of luxury imports and of elegantly crafted local goods.

Wheeler was looking in particular for signs of the Belgic first-century-BC chieftain Cassivellaunus, whose tribe, the Catuvellauni, produced several Celtic high kings of Britain, including Cunobelinus. It was Cassivellaunus, with his capital at Verulamium, who in 54 BC had led his people's resistance against Rome before succumbing to Caesar during the conqueror's second British foray. Wheeler found much of what he was after. On a plateau outside Verulamium's Roman walls, for example, he discovered a Belgic stronghold. Pottery dating from around 15 BC suggested that Cunobelinus's father, Tasciovanus, might have overseen the laying of the fort's foundations.

Running north and northeast of the hill fort were two earthworks from about the same pre-Roman period. Beyond these ramparts, near the town of Wheathampstead, Wheeler found the 90-acre site of a Belgic oppidum that turned out to be even older than his Verulamium find. Here potsherds, from native rather than imported ware, indicated a date toward the middle of the first century BC—the time of Cassivellaunus. The pottery, the huge ditches, and the earthworks on the site convinced Wheeler that it was at Wheathampstead that Cassivellaunus made his last stand against Caesar. Wheeler's exploration of an 11-acre site inside Verulamium's walls yielded some remarkable Roman finds, among them the foundations of a great gate that had spanned the entrance to its main road and a fine mosaic pavement with a scallop-shell motif.

The Verulamium excavations won admiring attention from the press, whose favor Wheeler was always careful to cultivate, since the coverage helped prompt public donations needed to finance his underfunded projects. At the end of it all, however, the archaeologist found himself still longing to uncover a British past beyond the Romans. "I suffered from a satiety of Roman things," he later wrote.

Their sides distinctively ridged by erosion and the tracks of generation after generation of grazing sheep, these gently rolling grassy hills form part of Maiden Castle, the largest Celtic hill fort in Britain. The British writer Thomas Hardy once likened this "stupendous ruin" to "an enormous many-limbed organism of antediluvian time lying lifeless and covered with a thin green cloth, which hides its substance."

"The mechanical, predictable quality of Roman craftsmanship, the advertised *humanitas* of Roman civilization, which lay always so near to brutality and corruption, fatigued and disgusted me." So in 1934 he turned from Verulamium and the "pretentious Roman machine" and fixed on another place to probe for Britain's pre-Roman Iron Age—Maiden Castle.

Situated in Dorset amid the grandeur of southern England's chalk hills, Maiden Castle was a challenge suited to Wheeler's venturesome nature. The huge, complex Iron Age settlement spread over 100 acres of a double-humped, saddle-backed spur. Some 47 acres alone lay within its elaborate defenses, which included three banks and two ditches with an extra bank running along most of the south side, and fortified entrances on the east and west. Even today, some of its ramparts rise nearly 60 feet high. The hill fort's name has nothing to do with maidens, but probably derives from the Celtic *mai-dun*—"Mai's fortress."

Mustering some 100 professionals and volunteers, the largest work force that English archaeology had ever seen, Wheeler would spend the the next four summers, between 1934 and 1937, at Maiden Castle, honing both his flair for publicity and the tactical talent that allowed him to derive maximum information from his work. It was there, for example, that he devised his ingenious grid system, which involved cutting the ground into a series of squares, each of which could be examined from all four sides *(page 136)*. Wheeler assured maximum publicity for his dig by setting up weekly press days that prompted a steady flow of feature stories; even an infant medium called television gave attention to the dig.

The results justified the coverage, for at Maiden Castle Wheeler succeeded grandly in reaching far back past the Romans. He found evidence of three Iron Age settlements, and beneath the first lay the remains of a Neolithic community that had existed 3,000 years before the first hill fort at Maiden Castle was founded. As for the successive hill forts, Wheeler concluded that the original one was built about 300 BC by farmers. After a century the Durotriges, a powerful tribe or confederation of tribes in southwest England, took over the site and made it into a formidable stronghold, greatly augmenting its defenses. A few generations later the fort was remodeled again in an even more ambitious and coherent way, this time, Wheeler the-

AN ARTIST VISUALIZES THE PAST

Wielding a pencil and sketch pad rather than a pick and trowel, English artist Alan Sorrell made lasting contributions to the archaeological history of Celtic Britain. Indeed, his impact has been likened to that of his colleague and contemporary the great archaeologist Sir Mortimer Wheeler, who did so much to uncover surviving traces of the Celtic past.

Shown above during a late-1950s sketching session at Stonehenge, Sorrell specialized in creating reconstruction drawings of ancient sites. In the words of one admirer, he gave "flesh and blood to the dry bones of archaeological reports." Sorrell made his first venture into archaeology in 1936, when he portrayed a Roman site in Leicester. The piece caught the eye of Wheeler, who asked Sorrell to do a reconstruction of the Roman assault on Maiden Castle, the hill fort Wheeler was excavating.

To prepare himself, Sorrell walked the area, talked to the archaeologists, and pored over maps, excavation materials, and photographs. Out of the endeavor also came the drawing below of the fort before the Roman conquest. Precise in its details, it takes the bird's-eye view typical of Sorrell's work. Sorrell came to master the aerial perspective for which he was famous when he served as an RAF airfield camouflager during World War II.

orized, by "a mastermind, wielding unquestioned authority and controlling vast resources of labor." The archaeologist believed this commanding genius to have been some minor Belgic prince who, with his followers, wrested control of the hill fort from the Durotriges and gave it its final pre-Roman form.

What was long believed to be evidence of Maiden Castle's final days had come to light some years before, in 1937, when excavations carried out by Wheeler turned up numerous skeletons, several of them showing signs of violent death *(page 137)*. These were, said Wheeler, the bones of Celtic defenders who had died in AD 43 during the onslaught of the Roman Second Legion led by Titus Vespasian, who would become Roman emperor in AD 69. From the physical evidence he found, Wheeler imaginatively described how Vespasian attacked the eastern entrance of Maiden Castle, his artillery laying down a barrage of arrows released from ballistae, or crossbows, in advance of an infantry charge up the slope. The fort was breached, and wholesale slaughter followed.

Some archaeologists today dispute Wheeler's reconstruction of the battle, even as they honor his archaeological methods and the valuable discoveries that make up his life's work. Among other things, they note that only 14 of the 52 skeletons examined show signs of violent death. Left unchallenged is the belief that Rome's takeover of England was, at least in part, a violent invasion, filled with dramatic battles.

Rome's interest in Britain began when Caesar first sailed there, citing a need to wipe out dissidents who were harboring anti-Roman refugees from Gaul and otherwise aiding their continental Celtic cousins. He was also probably interested in reports of mineral wealth on the island and in assessing the feasibility of a full-scale invasion later on. Bad weather and ship-

wrecks undermined both of Caesar's forays. Moreover, during the second venture tough opposition came from Cassivellaunus, high king of all of southern Britain. Cassivellaunus's highly effective guerrilla tactics and scorched-earth strategy caused the Romans no end of grief before the ruler was cornered, perhaps at the Wheathampstead site that Wheeler would discover almost two millennia later.

Deserted by some of his subordinate chieftains, Cassivellaunus surrendered, gave hostages to Caesar, and agreed to pay annual tribute to Rome. But troubles in Gaul aborted whatever further plans Caesar may have had for Britain, and he never returned there. In due course, Cassivellaunus regained his royal preeminence and forgot all about paying any tribute. And Britain returned to being an independent Celtic land. A century later, however, Rome—now transformed politically from republic to imperial power—turned its attention again toward Britain, prompted this time both by its usual territorial designs and by anti-Roman sentiment within the family of Cunobelinus.

The Celtic king began his long reign over a broad confeder-

The novel grid system introduced by Sir Mortimer Wheeler during his excavations at Maiden Castle is shown clearly in this 1936 view of the southern portal. The technique involved digging a series of squares, each at least 10 feet to a side and with enough uncut earth between them to accommodate a worker with a wheelbarrow—as well as the tourists who sometimes thronged the site. Each square afforded four cross sections of strata that could be studied and photographed.

ation of southern British tribes as a young man in about AD 10. Ruling from his fortified capital of Camulodunum, or modern Colchester, 55 miles from St. Albans, this exceptional ruler oversaw a period of remarkable prosperity in which Britain became a major commercial center. Its exports, according to Strabo, extended as far as Greece and Rome, and included cattle, wheat, gold, silver, tin, iron, and leather goods. In turn, Britain imported luxury items such as jewelry and wine from Europe. The coins that Cunobelinus minted in the Roman style, found during a dig at Colchester, show a stalk of wheat grown in the bountiful Essex countryside that he commanded. A grave unearthed at Lexden outside Colchester, rich enough to have been that of Cunobelinus himself, held a trove of magnificent imported objects befitting a king, such as chain mail with silver studs, silver tableware, a bronze table, statuettes, wine, high-quality pottery, jewelry, and objects of ivory and glass.

Cunobelinus kept the peace by assuring Rome of his friendship. Preoccupied with other parts of its empire, Rome left him alone. But toward the end of the fourth decade AD, as the king was getting old, two factions arose, headed by his sons. Adminius, attracted by Rome's riches and power, led a party that thought Britain would be better off within the empire. Two other sons, Togodumnus and his younger brother Caratacus, were fiercely anti-Roman. The upshot was that Cunobelinus banished Adminius, who promptly went to Gaul and petitioned Rome for help.

A Roman arrowhead, probably fired from a crossbow, is still lodged in the spine of a Celtic warrior whose skeleton was uncovered by Sir Mortimer Wheeler in a burial ground at the eastern entrance to Maiden Castle. The Celt was probably killed while defending the stronghold against a Roman onslaught in AD 43.

It was Adminius's misfortune that Rome's emperor at the time was the mad Caligula, an individual whose mental peculiarities were so pronounced that he would soon be assassinated by his bodyguards. In response to Adminius's request, Caligula broke off a campaign he was conducting against the Germans and marched his legions from Mainz all the way to the coast of Gaul, where he ordered them to attack the sea with their spears and swords. Afterward the troops were instructed to gather seashells as spoils of war and to rejoice in their mighty victory over Neptune, Rome's sea god. Unsettled, perhaps, at the prospect of alliance with this lunatic, Adminius stayed in Gaul and awaited developments in his homeland.

Sometime between AD 40 and 43 Cunobelinus died, and Caratacus and his elder brother Togodumnus succeeded him—a turn of events that gave the new emperor, the perfectly sane Claudius, a pretext to invade the island and enhance his reputation. He did not lead the invasion himself, however, but sent instead his general, Aulus Plautius, in command of four legions. The invasion force landed in AD 43 at what is now Richborough; meeting with no immediate resistance, it started inland.

Soon, however, Caratacus and Togodumnus began harrying Plautius in much the same way that their ancestor Cassivellaunus had bedeviled Julius Caesar a century earlier. The Celts might have done well to stick to that tactic; pitched battle was never their strong point, especially in Britain, where they still relied largely on chariot warfare long since obsolete in Gaul. But Caratacus decided to make a stand at the Medway estuary, reasoning that the Romans would have trouble crossing it without a bridge and could handily be cut down. It was a disastrous miscalculation. The Romans forded the passage with relative ease, at the same time executing a flanking maneuver that trapped the Celtic troops and inflicted upon them a stunning defeat. Togodumnus died later of wounds suffered in the battle, and Caratacus withdrew what remained of his army to Camulodunum, the British capital. Plautius followed.

With victory in sight, Claudius himself headed for Britain, bringing with him reinforcements, including a detachment of elephants that doubtless alarmed the Celts who had never before seen such beasts. He ordered Plautius to hold off taking Camulodunum, so that the victory over the Celts might be his. This gave Caratacus time to escape, along with his family and some followers. With the Celts seemingly in retreat, Claudius enjoyed a triumphal 16-day stay in Britain. Camulodunum became the capital of the new Roman province of Britannia, which took in all the agriculturally rich southern lowlands. The emperor received pledges of allegiance from several Celtic chieftains and dispatched part of the 20th Legion to build a fortress at Verulamium. Caratacus meanwhile headed west, to what is now Wales, to rally tribes there to continued resistance. In time, Adminius and a confederate named Berikos were set up as client kings in his place.

MYSTERY IN AN ENGLISH FARM FIELD

An ordinary field at Snettisham, England, has yielded treasure after Celtic treasure, yet no one knows why so much gold, silver, and bronze should have come to have been buried there.

The first discovery occurred in 1948 when a ploughman caught sight of a lump of metal and asked his foreman what it might be. Dismissing it as part of a brass bed, the boss tossed it aside. But after more metal fragments came to light, the piece was taken to the local museum and identified as a gold torque.

Excavations turned up additional torques in 1950, 1964, 1968, and 1973, including the eight-strand one at bottom right. But by 1973 the archaeologists assumed the field had nothing more to offer. Then, in 1989, an amateur archaeologist hit pay dirt with a metal detector: Scrambled together in a bronze cauldron was a collection of ingots, broken torques, bracelets, and other items, apparently scrap intended for melting *(top right)*. One of the torques, which had been lying wedged in the ground for 2,000 years, sprang back into shape as it was lifted from its resting place.

The archaeologists then launched an inch-by-inch examination of the field, and in the process of scraping away some six acres of topsoil uncovered five more hoards. Whoever buried

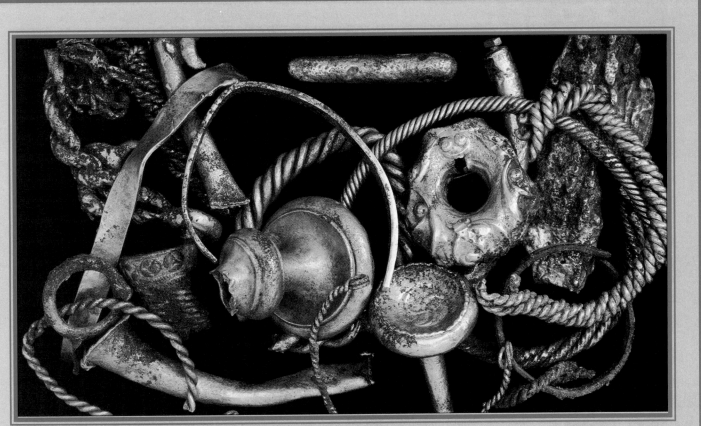

them took care to secrete three of them in double pits, the more precious pieces concealed in the bottom chambers. From the five hoards came no fewer than 63 complete torques. Gallo-Roman coins found with them have enabled archaeologists to date the treasure to around AD 70.

Further investigation has revealed a filled enclosure ditch ringing the 20-acre site. The circumscribed area must have had a special function, but in the absence of further clues, archaeologists can only theorize that it served as a burial place for votive offerings, or perhaps as a treasury or bank for the ruling house of the local Iceni tribe. Curiously, the enclosure was not located near any settlement. Taken together, the Snettisham hoards constitute one of the greatest Iron Age finds ever made in Great Britain.

With Claudius back in Rome, Plautius dispatched Vespasian to clean up the remaining resistance in southern Britain. The future emperor captured 20 fortresses during this campaign. Maiden Castle was one of them. Now Britannia's first governor, Plautius set about pursuing Rome's usual practice among its provinces of establishing client rulers to protect Roman interests and borders. He had little success in the Druid stronghold of western Britain and Wales and was forced to rely on his allies in the eastern part of the country, chief among whom was Cartimandua, queen of the Brigantes, a tribe occupying a large territory that now encompasses Yorkshire and Lancashire. No doubt Plautius would have liked some similar arrangement in Wales, but he failed to achieve it for a single reason: Caratacus was in Wales. The young king had recruited five tribes there in his anti-Roman cause. A stalemate held while Plautius stayed in Britain: As long as Caratacus remained quiescent, the governor left him alone. But in the fall of AD 47, Plautius's term was up, and a new governor, Publius Ostorius Scapula, arrived. Caratacus went on the offensive, resorting to time-honored Celtic guerrilla tactics and trying to avoid a major confrontation until he considered his forces strong enough. His successes prompted the Roman historian Tacitus to remark that the "natural ferocity" of the Celts "was intensified by their belief in the prowess of Caratacus, whose many undefeated battles, and even victories, made him preeminent among British chieftains."

Like Vercingetorix, however, Caratacus was doomed to fail. He could not avoid a pitched battle forever, and the confrontation came around AD 50, probably somewhere along the center portion of what is today the Welsh-English border. It was a fierce struggle, but in the end the Romans were victorious. As at Camulodunum, however, Caratacus and his family were once again able to escape the carnage. This time they fled north, seeking refuge with Cartimandua and the Brigantes. The choice was an unfortunate one. The wily queen knew that her future lay with Rome, and she betrayed her fellow Celt to Scapula, who had succeeded Plautius as governor. Caratacus and his family were taken in chains to Rome.

Once there, however, Caratacus managed to avoid the bloody end that Vercingetorix had met with. The British leader's fame had spread to Rome, and he was presented with great ceremony before

This 4⅛-inch-long bronze chariot fitting, in the form of a stylized horse's face, was found early in the 19th century with a hoard of horse and chariot gear in northern Yorkshire, once the domain of the mighty Brigantes tribe. Crafted sometime in the first century AD, the fitting may have graced the chariot of Celtic royalty.

Claudius, to whom he made a proud plea for clemency. As Tacitus reported it, Caratacus declared: "I had horses, warriors and gold; if I was unwilling to lose them, what wonder is that? Does it follow that because you desire universal empire, one must accept universal slavery?" The eloquent Celt also played upon the Roman respect for the judgment of history: "Were I dragged here as one who surrendered without fighting, no fame would have attached to my fate nor to your victory. If you punish me, they will both be forgotten. Spare me, and I shall be an eternal example of your mercy."

Claudius did spare him, and Caratacus and his family lived out their lives in Rome. Nevertheless, his defeat marked another milestone in the waning of the Celts.

Flanked by her daughters, a spear-bearing Celtic Queen Boudica gestures defiantly from her heavily armored, two-horse war chariot in this bronze statue erected in 1902 on the Thames embankment outside the Houses of Parliament in London. The work is more true to Victorian romantic notions than to Celtic realities: The deadly scythes on the chariot's wheels are pure invention, and Boudica would actually have ridden in a light, springy vehicle embellished with fittings like the one at left.

Even with Caratacus out of the way, Britannia refused to settle into the comfortable docility that Rome would have liked. Farther from Mediterranean influences than the Gauls, Britons continually chafed under the alien Roman administration and the high-handed manners of the imperial colonists among them. Moreover, the Romans seemed to deal with the new province even more tactlessly than with Gaul. For example, in Camulodunum they began building a temple to Claudius, using forced contributions from British chieftains to pay for this monument to Britain's conqueror.

A few years after Claudius was poisoned in AD 54, supposedly by his niece Agrippina, and her son, the 17-year-old Nero, became emperor, imperial troops violated the usual Roman policy of not tampering with native religions: They invaded Wales and attacked Anglesey, one of the most sacred of all Druid sanctuaries. Its significance to the Celts was underscored in the winter of 1942-1943 when the British air force was building a base there. Workers picked up and began using in construction what turned out to be a Druid slave chain with five neck rings, which once may have

bound the unfortunate victims of sacrificial rites. After the archaeologists were called in, a number of other Celtic artifacts came to light, including bronze ornaments and the remains of chariots, which verified Anglesey's position as a major cult center.

The kindling of discontent was torched into conflagration by an incident that took place in the land of the Iceni tribe of East Anglia. An uprising among the Iceni in AD 48 had prompted Rome to install a client king named Praesutagus, who had pledged his loyalty to Claudius. Before he died, Praesutagus bequeathed his kingdom to his two daughters jointly with the emperor. This was a common Roman way of saving an estate from total imperial confiscation, but it was a nicety seldom observed in the provinces, and in the case of Praesutagus's estate, Britannia's procurator, Catus Decianus, chose to ignore it. Decianus dispatched a group of underlings to the Iceni to make a full inventory of Praesutagus's holdings for expropriation by the empire.

These functionaries, however, ran afoul of Praesutagus's widow, Queen Boudica *(page 141)*. Much has been written about her feats over the centuries, and in the writing a series of clerical errors transformed her name to Boadicea, which passed into legend and is still known today. Her true name, Boudica, derives from the Celtic

Once thought by Sir Mortimer Wheeler to be the remains of victims beheaded during Queen Boudica's brutal sweep through Roman London, these skulls were among those unearthed during the 19th and early 20th centuries in the bed of London's old Walbrook Stream. Later study showed, however, that the skulls, most of which were male, bore no signs of violent death and in fact spanned several centuries. Some scholars now think they may have been used in rituals centering around veneration of water and the human head, carried on clandestinely while the Romans controlled southern Britain.

word for victory, *bouda,* and was the equivalent of Victoria. Queen Boudica objected to the confiscation of her family's holdings, and in retaliation the Romans stripped and flogged her and raped her daughters. This infamy prompted a national uprising, led by Boudica and involving almost all the British tribes. A notable exception was the Brigantes, led by the betrayer of Caratacus, Cartimandua, who, had she chosen to come to the aid of her fellow queen, might well have made a difference in the revolt's outcome.

As classical historians described her, Boudica at the head of her troops was an imposing figure, statuesque, fierce of countenance, her red-gold hair cascading to her hips. Outraged, she seemed to embody the fury now bursting forth in Britain, sweeping everything before it. In about 60 AD, the Britons assaulted and destroyed in quick succession the hated provincial capital at Camulodunum, then Verulamium, then Londinium (London), killing Romans and those Celts who were loyal to Rome. According to Tacitus, Boudica's soldiers behaved with unsurpassed barbarism, committing atrocities that included cutting off the breasts of women prisoners and stuffing them into their mouths, then impaling the victims lengthwise on stakes. In all, Tacitus says, 70,000 Romans and Roman sympathizers were killed in the sack of the three towns.

Ultimately, the Celts paid a high price for their uprising. Boudica's army was defeated, at a cost of some 80,000 British lives. The queen and her daughters killed themselves to avert further dishonor at Roman hands, and the Iceni were enslaved. Since the war had interrupted farming, famine swept the land, causing misery exacerbated by continuing persecution of the tribes that had rebelled. Gradually, however, over the next decade a restive peace set in as a new and more lenient governor took over, and Rome, shaken by the uprising, began treating Britain with a softer hand.

There was no more major warfare in the province of Britannia, although imperial forces did, in the early 70s, press farther into Wales and Yorkshire and into the north of Britain. A series of campaigns under the general Julius Agricola, between AD 78 and 84, pushed all the way into Scotland, where he defeated an army of Celtic Picts at Mons Graupius.

Rome was realizing, however, that there must be limitations for an empire to be effectively governed. In AD 122 the emperor

Hadrian ordered a 73-mile-long wall built across the island from the Tyne estuary to the Irish Sea. The great wall served two purposes: It protected the province from raids by the fierce Celtic tribes to the north, and it also delineated the extent of Rome's northernmost influence. In AD 162 the boundary moved north for a few decades as Antonius Pius had a second wall built, this one stretching from the Firth of Forth to the Clyde. South of the walls, the Romanization of Britain continued for a time.

But Rome itself was in decline. As early as the second century AD, Roman troops were being withdrawn from the province to defend parts of the empire closer to home, and around AD 407 the last of the Roman soldiers left. Romanized British chieftains began to reassert themselves; by now, however, their problems lay not to

As these three items demonstrate, Celtic artistic traditions persisted long after the Celts lost their political and military power. The bronze shield plate at far left, retrieved from the Thames near London in about 1855, dates from either the first century BC or AD; its gracefully swirling spiral and scroll motifs crop up on the cast silver-gilt Tara Brooch (left), *made in eighth-century Ireland. A page from the* The Book of Kells (right), *produced in the late 700s by Irish monks, expresses the curvilinear style at its fullest. The ornamented capitals are the first three letters of Christ's name in Greek.*

the south but to the north, where the Scots and Picts, who had never lived under Roman rule, pressed against them. And from the west came the Germans. By the fifth century Rome and what remained of its empire in the west were being overrun by Germanic tribes such as the Goths, Franks, Angles, and Saxons. Inexorably, in Gaul and Britain, the new invaders absorbed or displaced the Romano-Celtic populations.

The Celts did not vanish from history, although today the most visible traces in Europe are found in what is called the Celtic fringe: Ireland, Scotland, the Isle of Man, Cornwall, Brittany, and Wales. The combined population of these areas is only some 13 to 14 million people. And in this relatively small aggregation, Celtic languages are either dead or dying. The outposts where these tongues survive include western Ireland, where Irish is widely spoken, and Brittany, where about half the natives can speak Breton. About 26 percent of the Welsh speak Welsh, while only a little over one and a half percent of the Scots speak Gaelic.

It is indeed language that has distinguished the Celts for more than a thousand years, and it seems a curious twist of history that a people once restrained by custom and faith from writing things down would, when finally they took up the pen, produce some of the finest literature the world has ever known. It was the coming of Christianity and the concomitant demise of Druidism that freed the Celts to write. The new faith came to Ireland in the fifth century, and in due course the *scriptoria,* or writing rooms, of austere and remote monasteries filled with monks who spent their days copying and illuminating manuscripts. These works are best known for their sublime art, and the most famous of them is the *Book of Kells (page 145),* a rendering of the four gospels probably created in the ninth century at the island monastery at Iona, off the Scottish coast. It was taken from there to the Irish monastery of Kells in County Meath, most likely by monks fleeing from Viking raids. Christian though it is, the art of the *Book of Kells*—fluid, florid, intricate, a late blooming of the La Tène style—glows with pagan energy.

Despite their eye-straining labors over Scripture, Celtic Christian monks were not without some spare time, and they often used it to transcribe the folk tales and other lively vernacular literature that have come down to modern times. Given the wealth of their heroic

tradition, it is not surprising that it was also the Celts who gave the Western world one of its most important and enduring legends, the paradigm of chivalry found in the Arthurian tales.

The exemplar for King Arthur *(pages 130-131)* appears to have been a British chieftain who led the Celtic opposition to the invading Saxons around AD 500. In any case, by the sixth century the name Arthur was known and venerated throughout western Britain. The name turns up in the ninth century in a hodgepodge of folklore called *Historia Britonum,* compiled in Latin by a Welsh cleric named Nennius, and again in the 11th-century Welsh *Mabinogion,* a collection of mythic and heroic stories. Arthur reached a much wider audience in the 12th century when a Breton cleric living in Wales, Geoffrey of Monmouth, featured him in a fanciful concoction called *History of the Kings of Britain.* An amalgam of old stories, myth, and invention, the *History* formed the basis for the Arthurian tradition of brave knights and noble causes as the tale underwent numerous transmutations throughout the Middle Ages.

The ancient Celtic storytellers and medieval scribes have left as their progeny a lengthy roll of honor in Western literature: Jonathan Swift, Robert Burns, William Butler Yeats, George Bernard Shaw, James Joyce, Dylan Thomas, and Samuel Beckett, to name a few. And something less tangible has also been handed down: The Celtic passion for freedom at any cost. It was a legacy the Celts took with them on their last great migration, the exodus during the 18th and 19th centuries of so many Welsh, Scots, Irish, Cornish, Bretons, and Manx to North America, where their story is still being written, their contributions still being made.

In the grand sweep of history, the Celts of old have passed through twilight toward nightfall. But in the dawn of a rising appreciation of what they left behind, they flourish once more.

THE PEOPLE FROM THE BOG

According to the venerable parish register of Hermannsburg, a village in northwest Germany, peasants working in a bog more than 500 years ago chanced upon an unexpected and eerie sight—a man's body encased up to its neck in peat. Concerned that the deceased was deserving of a proper Christian burial yet no doubt frightened at the prospect of hauling a corpse out of the muck, they sought the advice of Magnus Lauenrod, their parish priest. Lauenrod, the chronicle relates, told them that the man's death must have been the work of elves and instructed the peasants to let the body be: Having lured the unfortunate man to his demise, the little people would soon also cover him up. And indeed, it appeared that the priest was right: When curious villagers returned to the spot the next day, nothing of the man remained to be seen.

The body's discovery and subsequent disappearance are common, say experts familiar with such so-called bog people. Countless numbers of similar ancient but well-preserved corpses have turned up over the centuries, including many apparently belonging to persons who lived during the Iron Age, yet very few were investigated scientifically. Most were probably simply covered up instead or, like the Hermannsburg man, left to feed the rodents, maggots, and foxes; others surely found their final rest in churchyards.

The Iron Age bodies shown on the following pages are exceptions, as are the flattened pair above. Known as Darby and Joan, the two were found in Werdingerveen, Holland, in June 1904. Examination revealed not only that Darby stood five feet ten inches tall but also that he likely died—ironically for a man with his right arm extended tenderly about the waist of a female companion—from a stab wound to the heart.

SACRIFICES TO THE FERTILITY GODDESS

Just as the seed is pushed deep into the soil, where it slumbers before awakening, so it appears that some of the bog people were ritually killed and then buried to ensure the success of the spring planting. Writing in the first century AD, the Roman historian Tacitus described one such ritual, performed every spring by an Iron Age Germanic people. In it, a priest symbolically marries the fertility goddess and rides with her on a cart through the countryside. Then the couple bathes in a "sequestered lake," and the goddess's attendants are sacrificed and "swallowed by that same lake." Tacitus made no mention of the priest's fate, but the number of garroted male bog bodies turned up to date suggests that he met with the same end.

A hemp noose fastened with a slipknot hangs around the neck of Borre Fen man (left), so named after the area in Denmark where peat cutters found him in 1946. His twisted 38-inch-long halter, pictured above, was probably used to choke him but may have been worn as an emblem of the fertility goddess, much as the gold torque at top would have been. Bogs have yielded dozens of such metal torques. Like Borre Fen man himself, the pieces are thought to have been tossed into the water as offerings to the goddess.

Tollund man (below) *was found in Denmark in 1950 lying on his side and wearing only a hide belt and a leather cap. A torquelike braided leather noose, likely used to choke him to death, was around his neck. Though the body was preserved well enough to determine the contents of his last meal—a gruel made of seeds—scientists chose to preserve nothing more than his head, shown freeze-dried at right.*

AN ADULTERER'S HARSH PUNISHMENT

Judging from various historical accounts, not all bog people were sacrificial victims. Some may have been violators of the strict and unforgiving code of conduct enforced by the Germanic tribes of the first century AD. "Traitors and deserters," Tacitus wrote, "are hanged on trees. Cowards, shirkers, and sodomites are pressed down under a wicker hurdle into the slimy mud of a bog." And a woman who had the misfortune to be accused of adultery, he reported, "is summarily punished by her husband. He cuts off her hair, strips her naked, and in the presence of kinsmen turns her out of his house and flogs her all through the village."

Such public humiliation may have preceded the death of the 14-year-old below, known as the

Windeby girl after the estate in Schleswig-Holstein, Germany, a province bordering Denmark, on which she was discovered in 1952 encased in peat. Except for an ox-hide collar circling her neck and a woven brown, red, and yellow blindfold covering her eyes, she was naked, and the hair on the left side of her head had been shaved short. Careful examination of her body revealed no sign of strangulation or other injury. The cause of her death, investigators concluded, was drowning.

The Windeby girl lies with the long birch branches that, together with a heavy stone lodged between her left arm and hip, were used to pin her beneath the watery surface of the bog.

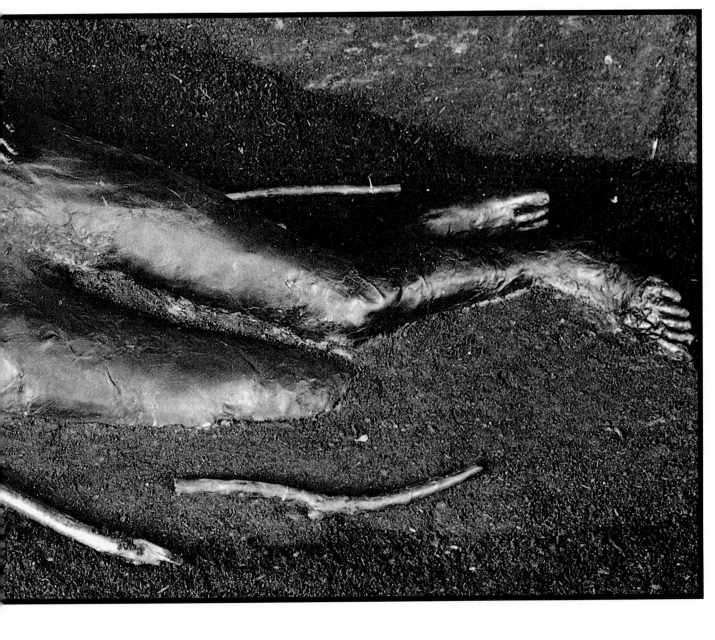

FEATS OF SELECTIVE PRESERVATION

The bog people owe their remarkable preservation to an event that occurred long before they lived—the retreat of the glaciers at the end of the last Ice Age. Across northern Europe, the British Isles, and elsewhere, the retreating ice left behind kettlelike depressions that gradually filled with water but drained poorly. The stagnant pools contained too little oxygen to support decay-causing bacteria. As a result, dead vegetation that fell into the ponds did not decompose readily and instead slowly accumulated to form peat—the component of bogs. On top of the ponds' quaking surfaces grew sphagnum moss and other hardy swamp plants. In addition to excreting antibiotics, the mosses raised the water's acidity, further retarding bacterial growth and setting the stage for tanning.

Provided that temperatures stayed cold enough, as they did in northern Europe through much of each year, the acids converted a body's outer layers into a leather that could last for centuries.

The 2,000-year-old woman at left was uncovered in Denmark in 1879 wearing some of the best-preserved Iron Age clothing ever found. As shown at right, a wool skirt reached to her ankles, and a sheepskin cape covered her torso and arms. Underneath was a second cape, made of lambskin, that she fastened over her left shoulder and secured with a leather strap.

A belt and a pair of leather shoes lie beside the remains of the man above, a freak of preservation turned up in a bog near Damendorf, in northern Germany. Strong acids in the water dissolved his bones and internal organs, leaving only an empty inch-thick bag of tanned skin, nails, and hair.

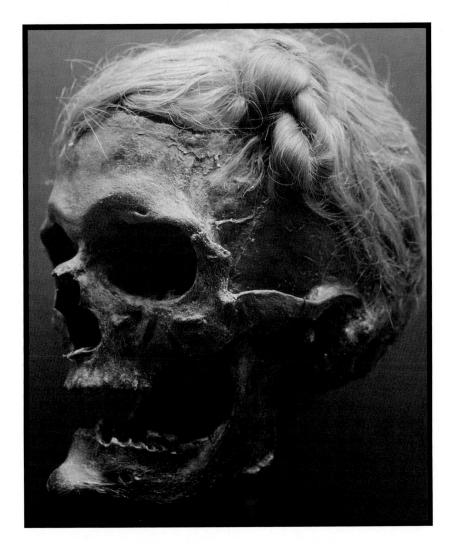

In contrast to Damendorf man, little skin or flesh remains on this male skull—only reddish blond hair that had been parted in the back and braided into a showy knot. Discovery of the head, in a bog southeast of Osterby, Germany, in May 1948, confirmed an account by Tacitus describing a similar hair style worn by an Iron Age Germanic tribe called the Suebi, ancestors of today's Swabians.

So well preserved was the skin of Grauballe man (right), found in April 1952 in a fen 11 miles east of Tollund, Denmark, with his throat slit, that criminology experts were able to take prints of the lines on his fingers and right foot, pictured here.

Though carbon-14 dating and pollen analysis confirmed that he died at least 1,500 years ago, a comparison of his prints with modern ones showed that he had the same loop pattern on his right index finger as more than two-thirds of Danish men today.

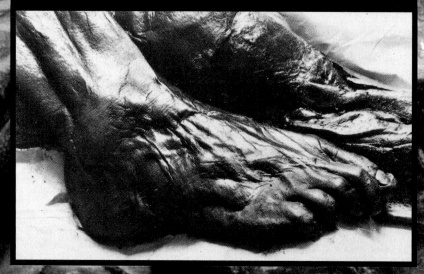

Centuries of exposure to tannic acid gave Grauballe man his shiny, leathery appearance, turned his two-inch-long hair an unnatural red-brown, and robbed his bones of calcium, making them soft. Yet the bog water also preserved his liver, lungs, testicles, and other organs. Investigators found eyeballs still in their sockets, and x-rays clearly revealed the two hemispheres of his compacted and shrunken brain.

THE SAGA OF AN IRON-WILLED PEOPLE

For more than 800 years, the remarkable Iron Age people known as the Celts held sway over much of Europe, the British Isles, and part of Asia Minor. Despite the vast sweep of territory their civilization encompassed, the Celts never developed a written language of their own or built a unified nation. Even so, they made great technological strides and produced artifacts noteworthy for their artistry, technical merit, and opulence.

The Celts probably descended from Stone Age peoples of Europe, who began to populate the Continent about 10,000 BC. Over the millennia, these hunter-gatherers gradually settled down to a life of cultivating crops and raising livestock. By 4000 BC, farming and cattle-raising communities had become dominant in much of central and northern Europe as well as in Britain. Within another 2,500 years, bronze- and metalworking techniques had spread from the Balkans to these lands as trade routes developed.

In the late Bronze Age, around 1200 BC, the Urnfield culture sprang up in parts of central Europe. Named for the custom of burying the ashes of their cremated dead in pottery urns, sometimes in large cemeteries, the Urnfield people gradually left their mark on the Rhine Valley, France, the Iberian Peninsula, northern Italy, and Britain. Accomplished metalworkers, they produced a variety of bronze goods, from farming and carpentry tools to finely wrought ornaments and heavy-duty weapons.

Around the start of the first millennium BC, a new culture took root and began to leave its traces. Skilled in bronzework, these Europeans eventually became masters of iron as the technology for smelting ore and fashioning the metal became available to them. Early Greek geographers referred to them in written works as the Keltoi. Scholars have divided Celtic history into the three overlapping phases discussed on the right.

HALLSTATT PERIOD
800-450 BC

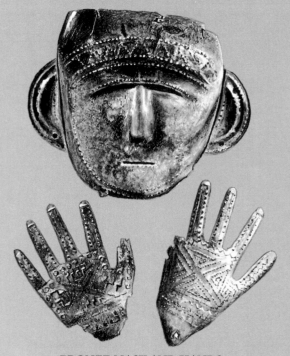

BRONZE MASK AND HANDS

The Hallstatt era was named for an Austrian village where a large early Iron Age cemetery was found. By around 800 BC, burials at this site had begun to shift from Urnfield cremation rites to inhumations. At about the same time, ironwork appeared in central Europe and iron weapons began edging out bronze in Celtic graves. As ironworking technology advanced over the next few centuries, so did Hallstatt culture, disseminated across the continent by traders, warriors, and migrants into the British Isles. A distinctive art style appeared, marked by simple yet strong geometric patterns, embellishing weaponry, tools, pottery, and ornaments. Elaborate burial items, such as the seventh-century bronze mask and hands above signaled not only the belief in an afterlife but also the development of a class structure, for these were tributes that only the well to do could afford.

By 600 BC iron was coming into regular use and commerce had joined agriculture and mining as a source of Celtic prosperity. Trade routes, which provided imports from the Greeks, Etruscans, and northern Europeans in exchange for such commodities as salt and iron, were dominated by an elite class of warlords ruling from hilltops or other strategically placed strongholds. Immensely rich, these chieftains took their fortunes—including imported luxury items and four-wheeled wagons—to their graves in wooden chambers that were covered by high mounds of earth. In the fifth century BC, perhaps because of disruptions in trade, many of the Hallstatt hill forts were abandoned and the wealth of this early period began to fade.

LA TENE PERIOD
450 BC-ROMAN CONQUEST

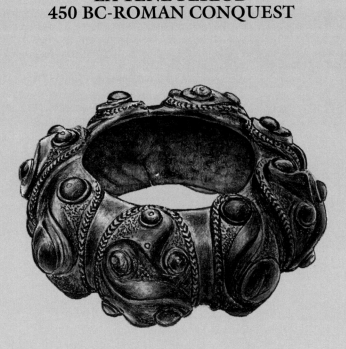

BRONZE ARMLET

ROMAN PERIOD
ROMAN CONQUEST-FIFTH CENTURY AD

LIMESTONE STATUE OF GALLIC WARRIOR

New centers of Celtic civilization had emerged by 450 BC. Increasing mastery of ironworking led to specialization, with such jobs as wagon maker, shipbuilder, wheelwright, and armorer coming into existence. Bands of fighting men left home to plunder and often settle in ever more distant lands. Two-wheeled chariots, rendered effective tools of war by their iron-rimmed wheels, graced the graves of warriors.

Amid this increased vitality an extraordinary new artistic style emerged. Dubbed La Tène (a label also applied to the second great phase of Celtic culture), it was named after a key archaeological site in Switzerland where a significant cache of artifacts had been dredged from a lake in 1857. Bold, curvilinear, and complex, La Tène design quickly became dominant throughout Celtic lands, adorning weapons and objects like the bronze bracelet above from the late third century BC.

Celtic affluence burgeoned as a result of revived trade and continual expansion as well as technological improvements in farming. Around 400 BC, Celtic tribes crossed the Alps, sacking Rome in 391 and settling down in northern Italy, which came to be referred to as Cisalpine Gaul. A century later, the Celts pushed into Greece and Asia Minor. By 250 BC, the dynamic La Tène culture was at its height, ranging from Italy to Ireland, from Spain to the Ukraine. In the absence of political unity, however, many settlements were plagued by intertribal strife.

The Celts resumed full-scale trading over their old trade routes, and by the beginning of the second century BC many of the hill forts of old had been replaced by newly established fortified towns. These oppida, as the Romans called them, served as centers of commerce and manufacturing. Immensely lucrative, Celtic trade grew increasingly dependent on Roman markets, even as Rome's emerging empire began pressing northward into Celtic lands.

In 192 BC Rome established its supremacy in Cisalpine Gaul and conquered, less than 70 years later, the area of southern France now known as Provence. By the mid-first century BC the Romans began their assault on western Europe. Led by Julius Caesar, Roman legions marched into Gaul in 58 BC. With their loyalties still tribal rather than national, the Celts were unable to mount a unified resistance, and in the ensuing fiercely fought battles lost much of their land. Six years later a leader named Vercingetorix rallied many of the remaining tribes in a pan-Celtic rebellion, only to be defeated at Alesia by Caesar in a fatal blow to La Tène culture on the Continent.

Gradually, the vanquished Celts adopted the ways of the victors, as evidenced by the limestone statue above, a late-first-century-BC portrayal of a Gallic warrior carved in the Roman style. Celtic culture remained dominant in Britain until AD 43, when the southern half of the island was conquered by Rome. Ireland then became the bastion of the Celts until its fifth-century conversion to Christianity. Even after that, tribal memories held onto Celtic languages and legends, which were at last written down by eighth-century Irish Christian clerics.

Cover: Réunion des Musées Nationaux, Paris. Background © British Museum, London. End paper: Art by Paul Breeden. 6: Prähistorische Staatssammlung, Munich, Foto Manfred Eberlein. 8-10: © British Museum, London. 11: © British Museum, London—The University of Liverpool Central Photographic Service; R. Davis, Bromley, Kent, England. 12: © British Museum, London. 14: © Erich Lessing, Culture and Fine Arts Archive, Vienna/Staatliche Museen zu Berlin-Preussischer Kulturbesitz, Antikensammlung, Berlin. 15: © British Museum, London. 16, 17: Gianni Dagli Orti, Paris/Musée de la Civilisation Gallo-romaine, Lyon, France. 19: Jean-Loup Charmet, Paris. 20: Museum of Natural History, Vienna. 22, 23: Museum of Natural History, Vienna; Dr. Lothar Beckel, Ischl, Austria. 24: © Erich Lessing, Culture and Fine Arts Archive, Vienna/Museum of Natural History, Vienna. 26: Photos et Recherches: Roger Agache. 28, 29: Musée Cantonal D'Archéologie Neuchâtel, Switzerland. 30: © Erich Lessing, Culture and Fine Arts Archive, Vienna/Fürstlich Hohenzollernsches Museum, Sigmaringen, Germany. 31: © British Museum, London. 33-41: Background Peter S. Wells, *The Emergence of an Iron Age Economy: The Mecklenburg Grave Groups from Hallstatt and Sticna.* American School of Prehistoric Research, Bulletin 33, figure 33. Copyright 1981 by the President and Fellows of Harvard College. 33, 34: Peabody Museum, Harvard University. 35: Peabody Museum, Harvard University, photograph by Hillel Burger. 36: Peabody Museum, Harvard University. 37: Peabody Museum, Harvard University, photograph by Hillel Burger. 38: Peabody Museum, Harvard University. 39: Peabody Museum, Harvard University—Staatliche Museen zu Berlin-Preussischer Kulturbesitz, Museum für Vor-und Frühgeschichte, Foto: Klaus Göken. 40: From Marie, duchess of Mecklenburg-Schwerin. *Prehistoric Grave Material from Carniola.* Sale catalog, compiled by Adolf Mahr. New York: American Art Association-Anderson Galleries, 1934. 41: Peabody Museum, Harvard University, photographs by Hillel Burger. 42: Mario Carrieri, Milan/Moravské Zemske Muzeum, Brno, Czech Republic. 44: © Erich Lessing, Culture and Fine Arts Archive, Vienna/Stuttgart Museum, Germany. 45: Konrad Theiss Verlag, Stuttgart. 46, 47: Dr. Hansjörg Küster, Vierkirchen, Germany. 48: J.-P. Mohen/Réunion des Musées Nationaux, Paris; J.-J. Hatt—Piero Baguzzi, Photo Service Fabbri, Milan/Musée Archéologique, Châtillon-sur-Seine, France. 49: Archives Tallandier, Paris—© Erich Lessing, Culture and Fine Arts Archive, Vienna/Musée Archéologique, Châtillon-sur-Seine, France. 51: © Erich Lessing, Culture and Fine Arts Archive, Vienna/Hallstatt Museum, Austria; © Erich Lessing, Culture and Fine Arts Archive, Vienna/Museum of Natural History, Vienna. 52: The Roman Site Museum, Corbridge/© English Heritage. 53: Alberto Bertoldi, Photo Service Fabbri, Milan/Museum Carolino Augusteum, Salzburg, Austria. 54: © British Museum, London. 57: Schweizerisches Landesmuseum, Zurich. 58: Musée Calvet, Avignon, France. 59: National Museum of Ireland, Dublin. 60: Projekt Heuneburg, Tübingen, drawing by Susanne Höfler, concept by Dr. Egon Gersbach. 61: Projekt Heuneburg, Tübingen. 62: The National Museum of Denmark, Copenhagen. 64: Piero Baguzzi, Photo Service Fabbri, Milan/Muzeul National de Istorie a Romaniei, Bucharest. 65: © Erich Lessing, Culture and Fine Arts Archive, Vienna/Musée Denon, Chalon-sur-Saône, S. et L., France. 66: © Erich Lessing, Culture and Fine Arts Archive, Vienna/Musée Borély, Marseille, France. 69: Prähistorische Staatssammlung, Munich, Foto Manfred Eberlein, courtesy National Museum, Prague. 71: Konrad Theiss Verlag, Stuttgart. 72, 73: From *The Celts,* © 1991, Gruppo Editoriale Fabbri Bompiani, Milan—Landesdenkmalamt Baden-Württemberg, Archäologische Denkmalpflege, Stuttgart (2)—Konrad Theiss Verlag, Stuttgart. 74: Landesdenkmalamt Baden-Württemberg, Archäologische Denkmalpflege, Stuttgart. 75: Landesdenkmalamt Baden-Württemberg, Archäologische Denkmalpflege, Stuttgart—Konrad Theiss Verlag, Stuttgart—drawing by J. Oellers, Landesdenkmalamt Baden-Württemberg, from *Der Keltenfürst von Hochdorf,* by Jörg Biel, Konrad Theiss Verlag, Stuttgart, 1985. 76, 77: Landesdenkmalamt Baden-Württemberg, Archäologische Denkmalpflege, Stuttgart; drawing by J. Oellers, Landesdenkmalamt Baden-Württemberg, from *Der Keltenfürst von Hochdorf,* by Jörg Biel, Konrad Theiss Verlag, Stuttgart, 1985—Volkmar Kurt Wentzel, © National Geographic Society; Konrad Theiss Verlag, Stuttgart. 78, 79: Landesdenkmalamt Baden-Württemberg, Archäologische Denkmalpflege, Stuttgart; Konrad Theiss Verlag, Stuttgart (2). 80, 81: Landesdenkmalamt Baden-Württemberg, from *Der Keltenfürst von Hochdorf,* by Jörg Biel, Konrad Theiss Verlag, Stuttgart, 1985—Landesdenkmalamt Baden-Württemberg, Archäologische Denkmalpflege, Stuttgart (2). 82: Dale M. Brown, Alexandria, Va. 84: Historical-Archeological Experimental Centre, Lejre, Denmark. 86, 87: Archives of the State Archeological Museum, Warsaw. 90, 91: © Erich Lessing, Culture and Fine Arts Archive, Vienna/Schweizer Nationalmuseum, Zurich; © Erich Lessing, Culture and Fine Arts Archive, Vienna/Keltenmuseum, Hallein, Austria—Piero Baguzzi, Photo Service Fabbri, Milan/Musée des Antiquités Nationales, Saint-Germain-en-Laye, France; Museum of Natural History, Vienna; © Otto Kasper, Singen, Hegau Museum, Germany. 93: The Danebury Trust, Institute of Archeology, Oxford. 94: © Butser Ancient Farm, Horndean, Hants., England. 95: Art by John Drummond, Time-Life Books—© Butser Ancient Farm, Horndean, Hants., England. 96: © Erich Lessing, Culture and Fine Arts Archive, Vienna. 97: Römisch-Germanische Kommission des Deutschen Archäologischen Instituts, Frankfurt. 98: Historical-Archeological Experimental Centre, Lejre, Denmark.

99: Drawing by F. Wyss, from *Die Kelten in Baden-Württemberg,* Konrad Theiss Verlag, Stuttgart, 1981. 100, 101: © Erich Lessing, Culture and Fine Arts Archive, Vienna/Musée Rolin, Autun, France; Werner Forman Archive, London/Musée Archéologique de Breteuil, France. 102: Prähistorische Staatssammlung, Munich. 103: André Held. 104: © Erich Lessing, Culture and Fine Arts Archive, Vienna/Museum of Natural History, Vienna. 105: © Erich Lessing, Culture and Fine Arts Archive, Vienna/Narodni Muzej, Ljubljana, Slovenia. 107: J.-L. Cadoux, Fouilles Université de Picardie, France. 109: © Erich Lessing, Culture and Fine Arts Archive, Vienna/Landesmuseum Joanneum, Graz, Austria. 111: © Mick Sharp, Caernarfon, Wales. 112: © Butser Ancient Farm, Horndean, Hants., England (2)—The National Museum of Denmark, Copenhagen. 113: © Mick Sharp, Caernarvon, Wales—© Butser Ancient Farm, Horndean, Hants., England (2). 114: © I. M. Blake and D. W. Harding—© Butser Ancient Farm, Horndean, Hants., England (3). 115: © Butser Ancient Farm, Horndean, Hants., England (2); © Mick Sharp, Caernarvon, Wales. 116, 117: © Butser Ancient Farm, Horndean, Hants., England. 118: Piero Baguzzi, Photo Service Fabbri, Milan/Musée Calvet, Avignon, France. 120: The Independent, London/Edward Sykes. 123: The National Museum of Denmark, Copenhagen. 124, 125: Werner Forman Archive, London. 126: The National Museum of Denmark, Copenhagen. 127: Timothy Taylor, Bradford, England; Archiv für Kunst und Geschichte/The National Museum of Denmark, Copenhagen—The National Museum of Denmark, Copenhagen; Karl Hoberg, Danish Police Forensic Science Laboratory, Copenhagen. 128: Explorer, Paris/R. Truchot. 129: Bibliothèque Nationale, Paris. 130: Piero Baguzzi, Photo Service Fabbri, Milan/Musée Vivenel, Compiègne, France. 131: © The British Library, London. 132, 133: Homer Sykes, London. 134: Mark Sorrell, Benfleet, Essex, England. 135-137: Dorset Natural History and Archeological Society, Dorset County Museum, England. 139, 140: © British Museum, London. 141: Collections London/Brian Shuel. 142: Museum of London/Archeological Services, photo by Edwin Baker. 144: © British Museum, London; © National Museum of Ireland, Dublin. 145: The Board of Trinity College, Dublin. 146, 147: Araldo De Luca, Rome/Musei Capitolini, Rome. 149: Drents Museum, Assen, The Netherlands. 150, 151: © Erich Lessing, Culture and Fine Arts Archive, Vienna/Museum für Vor-und Frühgeschichte, Saarbruecken, Germany—The National Museum of Denmark, Copenhagen (3); Ira Block, courtesy Silkeborg Museum, Denmark. 152: Archäologisches Landesmuseum der Christian-Albrechts-Universität, Schleswig, Germany. 154: The National Museum of Denmark, Copenhagen. 155: Archäologisches Landesmuseum der Christian-Albrechts-Universität, Schleswig, Germany. 156, 157: Ira Block, courtesy Moesgård, Århus, Denmark, Insets Moesgård, Århus, Denmark. 158, 159: Art by Paul Breeden.

ACKNOWLEDGMENTS

The editors wish to thank the following individuals and institutions for their valuable assistance in the preparation of this volume:
Roger Agache, Abbeville, France; Fritz Eckart Barth, Naturhistorisches Museum, Vienna; Marina Bertram, Staatliche Museen zu Berlin-Preussischer Kulturbesitz, Museum für Vor-und Frühgeschichte; Jörg Biel, Landesdenkmalamt Baden-Württemberg, Stuttgart; C. S. Briggs, Aberystwyth, Wales; Jean-Louis Cadoux, Faculté d'Histoire et de Géographie, Université de Picardie Jules Verne, Amiens; B. W. Cunliffe, Institute of Archeology, Oxford; Agnès Durand, Musée de la Vieille Charité, Marseilles; Helmuth Gann, Konrad Theiss Verlag, Stuttgart; Rupert Gebhard, Prähistorische Staatssammlung, Munich; Egon Gersbach, Institut für Ur-und Frühgeschichte, Projekt Heuneburg, Tübingen; Maria Grazia Giaume, R.C.S. Libri and Grandi Opere SpA, Milan; Gloria Polizzotti Greis, Peabody Museum, Harvard University, Cambridge, Mass.; Matthias Holzapfel, Bildarchiv Claus Hansmann, Munich; Marie-Louise Joffroy, Chatillon sur Seine; Ursula Kästner, Staatliche Museen zu Berlin; Wolfgang Kimmig, Institut für Ur-und Frühgeschichte, Projekt Heuneburg, Tübingen; Heidi Klein, Bildarchiv Preussischer Kulturbesitz, Berlin; Werner Krämer, Wiesbaden; Hansjörg Küster, Institut für Klassische Archäologie Universität, Munich; Daniel Melia, University of California, Berkeley; Herbert Melichar, Naturhistorisches Museum, Vienna; Rosalind Niblett, St. Albans, Hertfordshire; Fréderic Nowicki, Service Régional d'Archéologie, CDA, Amiens; W. Piotrowski, Archiwum Panstwowego Muzeum Archeologicznego, Warsaw; Marianne Rasmussen, Historical-Archeological Experimental Centre, Lejre, Denmark; Peter J. Reynolds, Horndean, Hampshire; Valerie Rigby, British Museum, London; Mark Scowcroft, The Catholic University of America, Washington, D.C.; Ian Stead, British Museum, London; Dominique Tisserand, Musée de la Civilisation Gallo-Romaine, Lyon; Rick Turner, Glamorgan, Wales; Carla Viazzoli, R.C.S. Libri and Grandi Opere SpA, Milan.

BIBLIOGRAPHY

The Age of God-Kings (TimeFrame series). Alexandria, Va.: Time-Life Books, 1987.

Allen, Derek F. *The Coins of the Ancient Celts.* Edited by Daphne Nash. Edinburgh: Edinburgh University Press, 1980.

Audouze, Françoise, and Oliver Büchsenschütz. *Towns, Villages and Countryside of Celtic Europe.* Translated by Henry Cleere. Bloomington: Indiana University Press, 1992.

Bacon, Edward (ed.). *The Great Archaeologists.* Indianapolis: Bobbs-Merrill, 1976.

Biel, Jörg. *Der Keltenfürst von Hochdorf.* Stuttgart: Konrad Theiss Verlag, 1985.

The Book of Kells. London: Thames and Hudson, 1980.

Brothwell, Don. *The Bog Man and the Archaeology of People.* Cambridge, Mass.: Harvard University Press, 1987.

Bruce-Mitford, Rupert (ed.). *Recent Archaeological Excavations in Europe.* London: Routledge & Kegan Paul, 1975.

Casson, Lionel. *The Barbarian Kings* (Treasures of the World series). Alexandria, Va.: Stonehenge Press, 1982.

Cavendish, Richard (ed.). *Man, Myth and Magic.* New York: Marshall Cavendish, 1983.

Coles, Bryony, and John Coles. *People of the Wetlands: Bogs, Bodies and Lake-Dwellers (Ancient Peoples and Places,* edited by Glyn Daniel). New York: Thames and Hudson, 1989.

Collis, John. *The European Iron Age.* New York: Schocken Books, 1984.

Cunliffe, Barry:
The Celtic World. New York: McGraw-Hill, 1979.
Danebury: Anatomy of an Iron Age Hillfort. London: B.T. Batsford, 1983.
English Heritage Book of Danebury. London: B.T. Batsford, 1993.

Daniel, Glyn. *A Short History of Archaeology.* London: Thames and Hudson, 1981.

Daniel, Glyn, and Paul Bahn. *Ancient Places: The Prehistoric and Celtic Sites of Britain.* Photographs by Anthony Gascoigne. London: Constable, 1987.

Dannheimer, Hermann, and Rupert Gebhard (eds.). *Das Keltische Jahrtausend.* Mainz: Prähistorische Staatssammlung München and Verlag Philipp von Zabern, 1993.

De Breffny, Brian. *Heritage of Ireland.* New York: Bounty Books, 1980.

Delaney, Frank. *The Celts.* London: BBC Publications, 1986.

Dimbleby, Geoffrey. *Plants and Archaeology.* London: Paladin, 1978.

Eluère, Christiane. *The Celts: Conquerors of Ancient Europe.* New York: Harry N. Abrams, 1993.

Empires Ascendant (TimeFrame series). Alexandria, Va.: Time-Life Books, 1987.

Evans, John G. *An Introduction to Environmental Archaeology.* London: Paul Elek, 1978.

Froncek, Thomas, and the Editors of Time-Life Books. *The Northmen* (Emergence of Man series). New York: Time-Life Books, 1974.

Glob, P. V. *The Bog People: Iron-Age Man Preserved.* London: Faber and Faber, 1969.

Hall, Jenny, and Ralph Merrifield. *Roman London.* London: The Museum of London, 1986.

Hansen, Hans-Ole. *The Prehistoric Village at Lejre.* Lejre, Denmark: The Historical-Archaeological Research Center, 1977.

Hatt, Jean-Jacques. *Celts and Gallo-Romans*. Translated by James Hogarth. Geneva: Nagel, 1970.

Hawkes, Jacquetta. *Adventurer in Archaeology: The Biography of Sir Mortimer Wheeler*. New York: St. Martin's Press, 1982.

Hencken, Hugh. *The Iron Age Cemetery of Magdalenska Gora in Slovenia* (Mecklenburg Collection, Part II). Cambridge, Mass.: Harvard University, 1978.

Jackson, Kenneth Hurlstone. *The Oldest Irish Tradition: A Window on the Iron Age*. Cambridge, Mass.: The University Press, 1964.

James, Simon. *The World of the Celts*. London: Thames and Hudson, 1993.

Jensen, Jørgen. *Guides to the National Museum*. Translated by Joan F. Davidson. Copenhagen: The National Museum, 1993.

Joffroy, René. *Vix et Ses Trésors*. Paris: Librairie Jules Tallandier, 1979.

Kaul, Flemming. *Gundestrupkedlen: Baggrund og Billedverden*. Copenhagen: Nyt Nordisk Forlag Arnold Busck, 1991.

Kimmig, von Wolfgang. *Die Heuneburg an Der Oberen Donau*. Stuttgart: Konrad Theiss Verlag, 1983.

King, Anthony. *Roman Gaul and Germany*. Berkeley: University of California Press, 1990.

Kruta, Venceslas:
Les Celtes. Paris: Hatier, 1978.
The Celts of the West. Translated by Alan Sheridan. London: Orbis, 1985.

Larsen, Erling Benner. *Moulding and Casting of Museum Objects: Using Siliconerubber and Epoxyresin*. Copenhagen: The Royal Danish Art-academy, 1981.

Lees, Duncan, and Aidan Woodger. *The Archaeology and History of Sixty London Wall*. London: The Museum of London, 1990.

MacCana, Proinsias. *Celtic Mythology* (Library of the World's Myths and Legends). New York: Peter Bedrick, 1987.

McIntosh, Jane. *The Practical Archaeologist: How We Know What We Know about the Past*. New York: Facts on File Publications, 1986.

Megaw, Ruth, and Vincent Megaw. *Celtic Art: From Its Beginnings to the Book of Kells*. New York: Thames and Hudson, 1989.

Moscati, Sabatino (coor.). *The Celts*. Milan: Bompiani, 1991.

Norton-Taylor, Duncan, and the Editors of Time-Life Books. *The Celts* (Emergence of Man series). New York: Time-Life Books, 1974.

Percival, John. *Living in the Past*. London: British Broadcasting Corp., 1980

Pernoud, Régine. *Les Gaulois*. Paris: Seuil, 1979.

Piggott, Stuart. *The Earliest Wheeled Transport: From the Atlantic Coast to the Caspian Sea*. Ithaca, N.Y.: Cornell University Press, 1983.

Pleiner, Radomir. *The Celtic Sword*. New York: Oxford University Press, 1993.

Powell, T. G. F. *The Celts*. London: Thames and Hudson, 1985.

Rajewski, Zdzislaw. *Biskupin: A Fortified Settlement Dating from 500 B.C.* Translated by Emma Harris. Poznan, Poland: Wydawnictwo Poznanskie, 1980.

Rankin, H. D. *Celts and the Classical World*. Portland: Timber Press, 1987.

Rees, Alwyn, and Brinley Rees. *Celtic Heritage*. New York: Thames and Hudson, 1961.

Reynolds, Peter J.:
Iron-Age Farm: The Butser Experiment. London: British Museum, 1979.
Life in the Iron Age. Minneapolis: Lerner Publications, 1979.

Ritchie, W. F., and J. N. G. Ritchie. *Celtic Warriors*. Aylesbury, England: Shire Publications, 1990.

Ross, Anne. *The Pagan Celts*. London: B.T. Batsford, 1986.

Royal Irish Academy. *Treasures of Ireland: Irish Art 3000 B.C.-1500 A.D.* Dublin: Royal Irish Academy, 1983.

Schutz, Herbert. *The Prehistory of Germanic Europe*. New Haven: Yale University Press, 1983.

Schwering, Axel von. *The Berlin Court under William II*. London: Cassell, 1915.

Sharkey, John. *Celtic Mysteries*. New York: Crossroad, 1975.

Sharples, Niall M. *English Heritage Book of Maiden Castle*. London: B.T. Batsford, 1991.

Sklenǎū, Karel. *Archaeology in Central Europe: The First 500 Years*. Translated by Iris Lewitová. New York: St. Martin's Press, 1983.

Sorrell, Alan:
Reconstructing the Past. Edited by Mark Sorrell. London: Batsford Academic and Educational Limited, 1981.
Roman Towns in Britain. London: B.T. Batsford, 1976.

Stead, I. M. *Celtic Art in Britain before the Roman Conquest*. London: British Museum Publications, 1985.

Stead, I. M., J. B. Bourke, and Don Brothwell. *Lindow Man: The Body in the Bog*. Ithaca, N.Y.: Cornell University Press, 1986.

Thorndike, Joseph J. (ed.). *Discovery of Lost Worlds*. New York: American Heritage, 1979.

Todd, Malcolm. *The Northern Barbarians: 100 BC-AD 300*. New York: Basil Blackwell, 1987.

Tresors Des Princes Celtes. Paris: Editions de la Réunion, 1987.

Turner, Rick. "Lindow Man and other British Bog Bodies." In *In Search of Cult: Archaeological Investigations in Honour of Philip Ratz*, edited by M. Carver. London: Boydell and Brewer, in press.

Warry, John. *Warfare of the Classical World*. London: Salamander, 1980.

Webster, Graham:
Boudica: The British Revolt against Rome, AD 60. Totowa, N.J.: Rowman and Littlefield, 1978.
The Roman Invasion of Britain. Totowa, N.J.: Barnes & Noble, 1980.
Rome against Caratacus: The Roman Campaigns in Britain, AD 48-58. Totowa, N.J.: Barnes & Noble, 1982.

Wells, Peter S.:
The Emergence of an Iron Age Economy. Cambridge: Harvard University Press, 1981.
Farms, Villages, and Cities. Ithaca, N.Y.: Cornell University Press, 1984.

Wertime, Theodore A., and James D. Muhly (eds.). *The Coming of the Age of Iron*. New Haven: Yale University Press, 1980.

Wilmott, Tony. *Excavations in the Middle Walbrook Valley: City of London, 1927-1960*. London: The Museum of London and the London and Middlesex Archaeological Society, 1991.

Wiseman, Anne, and Peter Wiseman.

Julius Caesar: The Battle for Gaul. Boston: David R. Godine, 1980.

PERIODICALS:

Bergquist, Anders, and Timothy Taylor. "The Origin of the Gundestrup Cauldron." *Antiquity,* March 1987.

Biel, Jörg:
"A Celtic Grave in Hochdorf, Germany." *Archaeology,* Nov./Dec. 1987.
"The Late Hallstatt Chieftain's Grave at Hochdorf." *Antiquity,* March 1981.
"Treasure from a Celtic Tomb." *The National Geographic,* March 1980.

"Chieftain's Burial at St. Alban's." *The Colchester Archaeologist,* No. 6, 1992-1993.

Fitzpatrick, A. P. "The Snettisham, Norfolk, Hoards of Iron Age Torques: Sacred or Profane?" *Antiquity,* Vol. 66, 1992.

Hencken, Hugh. "How the Peabody Museum Acquired the Mecklenburg Collection." *Symbols,* Fall 1981.

Keys, David. "Charred Remains Hold Clues to a Celtic Collaborator." *The Independent,* April 1, 1992.

Lane, Steve. "Celtic Treasure from Norfolk." *Minerva,* May/June 1991.

Larsen, Erling Benner. "The Gundestrup Cauldron Identification of

Tool Traces." *Royal Art Academy,* Copenhagen, n.d.

Marsh, Geoff, and Barbara West. "Skullduggery in Roman London?" *Transactions of the London and Middlesex Archaeological Society,* 1981.

Niblett, Rosalind. "A Catuvellaunian Chieftain's Burial from St. Albans." *Antiquity,* Vol. 66, 1992.

Raftery, Barry. "The Celts: The First Europe." *Minerva,* July/Aug. 1991.

Smith, Donald. "Did King Arthur, Camelot Exist?: Archaeologists Debate Evidence." *The Buffalo News,* August 22, 1993.

"Snettisham." *Current Archaeology,* No. 135, Aug./Sept. 1993.

Stead, I. M. "The Snettisham Treasure: Excavations in 1990." *Antiquity,* Vol. 65, 1991.

Taylor, Timothy. "The Gundestrup Cauldron." *Scientific American,* March 1992.

Wainwright, G. J., and B. W. Cunliffe. "Maiden Castle: Excavation, Education, Entertainment?" *Antiquity,* Vol. 59, 1985-1986.

Wells, Peter S.:
"The Excavations at Sticna in Slovenia by the Duchess of Mecklenburg, 1905-1914." *Journal of Field Archaeology,* Summer 1978.

"Prehistoric Charms and Superstitions." *Archaeology,* May/June 1984.

OTHER SOURCES:

Bökönyi, Sándor. "Mecklenburg Collection, Part I: Data on Iron Age Horses of Central and Eastern Europe." Bulletin 25. Cambridge, Mass.: Peabody Museum, 1968.

Greis, Gloria, and Michael Gezelowits. "The Mecklenburg Collection: European Archaeology at Harvard's Peabody Museum." Unpublished exhibit notes. Cambridge, Mass.: Peabody Museum, 1988.

Kroon-Voordracht, Vijfde. "Air Photography and Archaeology: Achievements and Prospects." Amsterdam: Netherlands Museum, 1981.

Marie, duchess of Mecklenburg-Schwerin. *Prehistoric Grave Material from Carniola.* Sale catalog, compiled by Adolf Mahr. New York: American Art Association-Anderson Galleries, 1934.

Wilhelm, Kaiser:
"Letter to Duchess of Mecklenburg." Cambridge, Mass.: Peabody Museum, June 18, 1913.
"Letter to Duchess of Mecklenburg." Cambridge, Mass.: Peabody Museum, Feb. 8, 1914.

INDEX

GOLD BOAT

NORTH SEA

Gundestrup

Tollund

Windeby

Lindow
Moss

Snettisham

HOCHDORF
FIGURINE

St. Albans

Danebury
London
Butser

Maiden Castle

Rhine River

Ribemont

GAUL

ATLANTIC OCEAN

Finistère

Seine River

Loire River

Hochdor

Heuneburg

Avaricum

Alesia

Vix

Saône River

Lake
Neuchâtel

BOAR HUNT

Bibracte

Coligny

La Tène

VERCINGETORIX COIN

Gergovia

ALPS

Rhone River

Po River

Marseilles

IBERIA

MEDITERRANEAN SEA